CULTURAL HERITAGE AND CONTEMPORARY CHANGE
SERIES I, CULTURE AND VALUES, VOLUME 28
SERIES IV. WESTERN EUROPE, VOLUME 4
General Editor
George F. McLean

Speaking of God

Carlo Huber, S.J.

THE COUNCIL FOR RESEARCH IN VALUES AND PHILOSOPHY

Box 261
Cardinal Station
Washington, D.C. 20064

BT
103
. H83
2001

Printed in the United States of America

Library of Congress Cataloging-in-Publication

Huber, Carlo.
    Speaking of God / Carlo Huber.
    p. cm. -- (Cultural heritage and contemporary change. Series I,
Culture and values; vol. 24) (Cultural heritage and contemporary change.
Series IV, West Europe; vol. 4)
    Includes bibliographical references and index.
    1. God. 2. Philosophical theology. 3. Language and languages--
Religious aspects--Christianity. I Title. II. Series. III. Series : Cultural
heritage and contemporary change. Series IV; West Europe, vol. 4
BT103 .H83 2001
231'.01'4--dc21   2001005387
                                                                  CIP

ISBN 1-56518-169-7 (pbk.)

CONTENTS

INTRODUCTION

This is a book of philosophy; its development follows the lines of the philosophical methods known in linguistic analysis and phenomenology. However these philosophical methods are employed here in consideration of a theological problem: the meaningfulness and reasonability of that which Christians say about God.

Obviously, such a philosophical undertaking is fraught with problems. Does philosophy have the capacity to comprehend theological matters, matters which rely on divine revelation? What authority does philosophy have on questions of the significance and the reasonability of faith and of theological argumentation? Apparently none!

However, since we human beings are capable of understanding what God has revealed, even if not with complete, interior comprehension, divine revelation must occur in human language and must thus be accessible to the general tools of linguistic analysis and logic, as well as to those of a phenomenology of the contents of human consciousness. Moreover, the material object of philosophy is unlimited: all of actual and possible reality – "being qua being". Logic too can and must occupy itself with every argumentation. Certainly there are precedents for a philosophical treatment of theological issues; it suffices to recall not only Augustine and Aquinas, but also Maimonides, and the Arab theologians of the Middle Ages; in modern times Hegel, and in our own century Ricoeur, Levinas, and Rosenzweig.

However, philosophy can consider a theological issue only if it is permitted to approach the issue as it would approach any other issue; philosophy cannot *presuppose* truth on account of divine revelation. At the same time, philosophy must respect the specificity of the theological terrain — as we shall see.

We intend to discuss the significance and reasonability of that which Christians say about God in general, in a broad sense. We need however to distinguish two levels of Christian discourse about God. On the one hand, a part of what Christians say about God is common , in some form, to other religions as well and as such has been considered philosophically from the time of Plato, Aristotle, Plotinus and others. However, another part of Christian discourse is born exclusively of revelation, as when we speak of the Trinity or the Incarnation. Clearly these two 'parts' cannot be legitimately separated; revelation as such has always been ingredient in the philosophical reflections of Christians, and the way in which a Christian speaks of God is, in the concrete instance, always seamless. Precisely for this second reason the object of our philosophical endeavor here is Christian discourse in the broadest, 'global' sense – a 'given' which is specific, historical, religious, Christian, and in some fashion already theologically elaborated.

This book is articulated in three parts, for which I have chosen three articulations of philosophical reflection upon wittgenstein.

The *first part*, chapters 1 to 3, is a **semantics** of religious language.

The *second*, chapters 4 to 6, considers a **logic** of Christian discourse on God.

The *third* and final part attempts a **pragmatics** of the faith.

The *philosophical methods* employed in our analysis of Christian discourse are: first, that of logical-linguistic analysis, referring back to Ludwig Wittgenstein and predominating in the first five chapters; and second, that of phenomenological reduction, adopted in the sixth and seventh chapters and deriving from Edward Husserl.

But before we introduce the methods of our analysis we need to speak further of the object of the analysis — the philosophical facticity of Christian discourse about God.

PART I

A SEMANTICS OF RELIGIOUS LANGUAGE

CHAPTER ONE

CHRISTIAN DISCOURSE ON GOD

A NEGATIVE DELIMITATION

'Religious language in general' does not exist. Religious language is found only in a concrete and historical form, whether Greek, pagan, Buddhist, Islamic, Jewish, or, as in our case, *Christian* discourse. The generalized 'religious discourse' referred to by philosophers of religion is an abstraction performed upon the material of concrete instances of religious discourse. The question arises whether this abstraction takes *all* religions into account or rather has been based upon certain religions selected according to certain criteria. And it is also possible that the abstraction has been *constructed* — an 'ideal' religious or pseudo-religious discourse along *humanistic*, illuministic or idealistic lines, possessing a certain number of similarities with concrete religious discourse. Moreover, the term 'religious language' is sometimes used to refer to the 'meta-language' in which one speaks about diverse forms of concrete religious language.

But here we are concerned neither with the variety of concrete extant or historical religions such as Buddhism. Islam, Hebrew, Greco-pagan, etc., nor with 'religious discourse in general', but rather with the form of religious language in which Christians, and specifically, practicing Roman Catholic Christians, express themselves.[1] This is by *no* means intended as an exclusion of the way in which religious discourse is used by other Christian confessions or denominations. Between the language of Catholics and, for example, Lutherans, there are interesting differences of style, of argumentation, and of historical-cultural connections. From a logical and structural point of view these differences are minimal when compared with the differences which occur between the religious speech of Christians and the religious speech of non-Christians. Nevertheless they do make themselves felt.

A POSITIVE DELIMITATION

Religious discourse consists in that which Christians say both institutionally and *de facto* about God. We can 'deduce' neither philosophically nor theologically *what* religious speech is or what is its essence. We don't even want to propose a definition. We will not say, "religious language should be this way . . .", or: "One ought to speak thusly. . . ." Here we want simply to see how people, and specifically how Christians, use language in the context of their faith, i.e., when practicing their religion. (This does not of course exclude the 'normativeness' imparted by *the rules* of a specific religious discourse, especially Christian discourse – a normativeness which in any event is essential to *any* language.)

We have to ask: "What is a 'religious' use of language? What is a religious practice? What is a religious context?" In this case we are asking Christians how they use the word 'religion', the word 'faith', or other terms that refer to the same thing. What *for them* makes a situation, a context, a practice *'religious'*?

When a Christian speaks, he does not always use the language of his faith, though he might well make the claim that his entire life is, or ought to be, a life of faith, a life of testimony to the faith, etc. But *linguistically* this faith does not make itself continuously apparent, anymore than it does behaviorally. It can be the case that the daily language of a Christian is more or less colored by his being Christian. Nonetheless, not all daily speech can qualify as religious discourse. In particular, scientific speech and technical discourse — engaged in of course also by Christians — are wholly free of any religious shadings; it is simply illegitimate to import elements of religion into a strictly scientific or technical discourse. To be sure, there are borderline instances, but the man or woman forever giving a religious coloration to any and every subject of daily speech is generally considered strange, bigoted, boring and perhaps fanatical.

It is an easy matter to tick off some *typical cases of the religious use* of language on the part of a Christian: to preach and to listen to a homily, to make a profession of faith, to participate at the Liturgy, to pray publicly with others or privately, aloud or in silence, to teach religion and to take a course in religion, to speak of the faith and discuss it with others, also with non-believers, to study or teach theology, and so on. It is also an easy matter to list some typical cases which no Christian would spontaneously classify as 'religious': to go over one's accounts, to teach mathematics, to ask the time, to play ball. . . .

However there are the borderline cases. These include expressions originally Christian but absorbed into the general linguistic-cultural baggage and now used not only without thinking about the origins, but often without even knowing them: local place-names (San Francisco), names of persons and of things, farewells (God be wi'ye = good-bye), curses. Indeed, borderline cases exist precisely because the borders of the various linguistic games are *not* fixed, and even the borders themselves depend on *use*. The words: *religion, faith,* etc., like the majority of words in fact, do not have a unique and 'fixed' meaning, but rather a certain 'fuzziness' around the edges. Thus even the significance of 'religion', 'faith', 'Christian', 'language', 'religious language', 'Christian discourse', etc.,[2] is to be determined by the institutional *use* of these words within a given linguistic community,[3] and not by means of a definition of their singular 'essences'. We can for the moment then leave aside the question of whether and how far the word 'religion' is applicable to Confucianism, Buddhism, or to a religious 'feeling' purely interior and private, to a conviction of the existence of God which is purely philosophical ("natural religion"), to humanitarian and socialistic ideologies, etc.[4] It has to be said that their respective discourses bear a resemblance among each other and also with the discourse that is used in the context of the great religions, including Christian discourse. However there are also noteworthy differences, of which we will speak in Chapter 3.

THE FACTICITY OF THE *LINGUISTIC* RELIGIOUS BEHAVIOR OF CHRISTIANS

Every method, every reflection, every type of philosophical endeavor must have a *datum* to which it is then applied. In our specific case the datum to be considered consists in the social and historical reality of the religious linguistic behavior of the Christian, i.e., in the language actually used and spoken by Christians in the context of their faith. This behavior is describable and analyzable not only by sociology but also by philosophy — which is to say, by logic, phenomenology, and existential analysis.

But we need first to pose a preliminary question here. *Who*
engages in Christian religious discourse? Who are the Christian
Catholics? This question too is to be treated in the same way as our
preceding question, 'What is religion?' In other words, *how* are the
words 'Christian' and 'Catholic' *used* in our language?

Normally it is clear that one is a Christian when one acts
and speaks as one. And it is quite evident that the *amplitude* of the
terms 'religious', 'Christian' and 'Catholic' gradually narrows. One
cannot legitimately use the term 'Christian' without a historical
reference to Christ. Moreover the term "Catholic" is employed
almost exclusively today to refer to an organized and institutional
group of Christians which is called the "Catholic Church."[5] It would
appear to be legitimate also for this group to declare in a normative
way: "This person has (or does not have) the right to call himself
'Catholic'; this doctrine or behavior is Catholic (or is not)." Of course
here too we encounter fuzziness around the edges. Whether or not
a 'Christianity without religion', an 'atheistic belief in Jesus', a
'Catholicism without the power structure',[6] are still to be called
'Christian' or 'Catholic' is a question of linguistic use and therefore
a question of convention, and thus often a pedagogical, polemical,
and political matter of no small importance.

Thus it is clear that the datum of Christian discourse about
God is a *positive, historical, socially shared, institutional* and in
some way *supernatural* datum. This *fact* is the subject of our
linguistic analysis here.

Christian Discourse about God — a Positive Fact

The *datum* ("that which is given") of any philosophical
reflection always precedes the philosophical reflection itself, and
the same holds with regard to an analysis. If nothing is 'given' to
me, then I have nothing to analyze, nothing on which to reflect,
nothing to order, organize or systematize. The 'data' of philosophical
reflection as such are not the product of that philosophical reflection.
In this sense, philosophy, of whatever branch, always and necessarily
begins *a posteriori*.[7]

Christian Discourse on God is a Historical 'Given'

A language or a speech form, in our case, religious/Christian/ Catholic speech, is a reality that is born and develops *historically.* It is *not* developed according to logical rules, nor according to a project conceived of *a priori,* nor within the Divine Mind.[8] In a philosophical analysis we must accept Christian-Catholic discourse in its *accidental* and historical concreteness. Perhaps it might have developed differently, but in fact it developed as it did. This actually-existing speech is the only speech which interests us because it is the only one which is 'given' us. Considering that its existence is historically contingent, there is always the possibility that in the future it will take another direction,[9] but to us it is 'given' in the form in which it has developed to date. What 'could be' or 'will be' is not yet given to me, and therefore I am not able to analyze it.

For the analysis of a particular form of discourse, especially of the religious-Christian kind, one must take into consideration the way in which this speech form arose and how it developed historically. Nevertheless the *meaning* of a linguistic expression consists not in its origin, nor in its development, its history or its etymology, but in its *actual use.* (And here, in the comprehension of its actual use, the history of a linguistic expression can be of considerable assistance.)

For an understanding of religious-Christian discourse, we need to recall that this discourse has its 'normative' origin in scriptural speech – in the Old and, even more to the point, the New Testaments.

One additional point in the context of the historical givenness of Christian-Catholic discourse: the *normative* truth of the dogmas of the faith is to be understood according to the *historical linguistic usage* of the times in which a particular dogma was formulated.

Christian discourse about God is a social given

No language, no speech form, no mode of speaking is purely personal. The *use* of a linguistic expression — that which determines the expression's significance — is its *use in the language.*[10] i.e., how an expression *is* used, and not how *I* use it. This applies not only to a natural language but to every type of speech form — to the terminology of physics, of mathematics, medicine, of logic, and of philosophy itself. The religious/Christian/Catholic forms of speech are among the speech forms especially determined by their history, insofar as there is no possibility of *indicating* the objects which they are to signify, i.e., God, grace, etc.; in addition, Christians, and especially Catholics, in using their religious language, understand one another as a community, as 'Church'. This is to say that they understand one another *insofar* as they practice their religion and communicate in their religious language.

Christian discourse about God is an institutional given

This point merely amplifies the preceding one.[11] The different languages, and especially the various forms of discourse, which differ historically, culturally and socially, are a reality which *institutionally precedes* the actual use to which a speaker puts them. Indeed a given speaker creates neither his language nor his various speech forms but learns them — because they are already spoken. The individual learns not only his mother tongue but also a variety of special forms of discourse – Christian-Catholic discourse, for example in a process of linguistic socialization. These tongues and speech forms already exist, which is to say, they are already spoken. The individual human being acquires these languages precisely in the manner in which they are already spoken. Only as a consequence is it possible to make of *this learned speech form* a personal use, given that human speech is fundamentally open and elastic.

The human being cannot speak if not by using languages and speech forms already existing actually, and using them in the way in which these are *institutionally used*. This is to say that the human being cannot speak, giving a significance to what he says such that others can understand and such that he himself knows what he says, except by using the language according to its particular *common rules*. Anyone can of course speak in a personal fashion, in an individualized style, even inventing new words. But this very individualized speech is possible only in dependence upon an institutional language already existing. Personalized speech is something that must be *acquired* in the using of a language.

At the same time, a speech form is clearly not an immutable reality. Language changes, develops and is transformed. Human beings themselves change it – but in the plural. An individual, separated from all others, divorced from the linguistic community, could never introduce a linguistic change. Moreover, even the evolution of a language takes place according to rules.

Christian discourse about God is a 'supernatural'[12] given

For a Christian, not only does Christian religious discourse have a historical origin but this historical origin is determined by the *specific* intervention of God, who is the *causa principale*. Certainly, the biblical and therefore 'supernatural' aspect of Christian discourse regards its *contents,* and not so much its expression or semantics, nor its logic. But here again, the border between these two aspects cannot be very sharply drawn.

We can say this much: in applying ourselves philosophically to a datum which is, theologically, a supernatural datum, we are not committing a methodological error. It is indeed rare that the datum of a philosophical analysis is itself a philosophical datum. On the other hand, we cannot presuppose that Christian discourse is in fact a supernatural datum, nor can we 'take it on faith' that that which Christians say about God *is true,* and we certainly do not intend to *demonstrate* it. We must however take into consideration as simply a *fact,* that Christians consider that which they say about God *as true,* because that is a part of the 'givens' of their discourse, of the significance of what they actually say.

NOTES

1. Here, "practicing Catholics" means specifically: those who attend Mass regularly, pray regularly, and attempt to deepen their faith. This is not without significance, for simple baptism and a childhood aquaintance with the catechism do not at all guarantee a competent use of religious language and, without continual practice, can lead to linguistic deformations.

2. See Chapter 3.

3. Cfr. Ludwig Wittgenstein, *Philosophical Investigations*

(PU), n. 43.

4. We can recall here the 'religion of Reason', proclaimed by the French Revolution, the 'positive religion' put forth by Comte, and the 'Positive Christianity' of Hitler and Rosenberg.

5. Originally, and until the Protestant Reformation, the term 'Catholic' meant simply 'universal'.

6. Cfr. Carlo Huber, S.J., "Christianismo senza Dio," in *Christiano oggi,* ed. Paoline (Rome 1977), pp. 91-118.

7. For this reason philosophy was known as the 'scientia verspertina'.

8 We must be careful not to think of the Divine Intellect as a computer or a Super Brain!

9. The specifc limits upon the possibility of developement and change in Christian/Catholic discourse are considered in K. Huber, *Critica del Sapere* 8.313, pg. 155f.

10. Cfr. Wittgenstein, PU 43.

11. Cfr. However, Huber, *Critica del Sapere,* 8.3, pp. 153-159.

12. 'Supernatural' here is not intended to signify 'miraculous' nor does it refer to one of the many theological theories of 'the supernatural'.

CHAPTER TWO

THE PHILOSOPHICAL METHODS OF OUR DISCUSSION

Logical Analysis and Phenomenological 'Reduction'

To the object of our discussion, Christian discourse about God as we have determined it in the preceding chapter, we will be applying primarily two philosophical methods – linguistic analysis as elaborated by Ludwig Wittgenstein in the *Philosophical Investigations*, and phenomenological 'reduction' as developed by Edmund Husserl. Given the intricacy of these two methods we need first to explain the methods themselves and call attention both to their potential and to the limits of their specific usefulness for an analysis of the Christian discourse about God.

I. LOGICAL ANALYSIS OF LANGUAGE: LUDWIG WITTGENSTEIN, 1889-1951

To speak about Wittgenstein and his philosophy means to speak about speech, about the philosophy of language, and specifically about linguistic analysis — a philosophical movement that has profoundly conditioned today's philosophical climate. At the same time, to speak about linguistic analysis as a philosophical 'method' means to speak principally of Wittgenstein. To be sure, not all of the philosophers who practice linguistic analysis follow Wittgenstein strictly. An approach or style closely resembling Wittgenstein's would be difficult indeed, given the elasticity and non-systematic character of Wittgenstein's second period of philosophical development. However all the philosophers who engage in linguistic analysis have come under the influence of Wittgenstein in one way or another: the Vienna Circle and Neopositivism in general were inspired by the *Tractatus* Logico-Philosophicus. The "Common Language Philosophy" of Ryle, Austin, and others was at least in part stimulated by Wittgenstein's manuscripts, the "Blue Book" and the "Brown Book", which circulated among Cambridge and Oxford students during the 1930's and 40's. All of the current research and publications in the field of linguistic analysis stand under the influence of the *Philosophical Investigations.*

As we shall see, the analytical method of this work of Wittgenstein's second period is not a part of a philosophical system; indeed its method is resoundingly *anti-systematic.* Moreover the method itself is quite complex, as we also shall see.

Even generally speaking, one does not truly *comprehend* a method unless one knows how it relates not just to one single area or field but to a variety of fields. This general rule becomes especially true in the case of the analytical method of the *Philosophical Investigations.* Since we will be making frequent use of this method during the course of our analysis of the way in which Christians speak about God (indeed, we have employed it already in Chapter One), we need to examine that method in some detail. This obliges us also to look, if only briefly, at the *systematic* philosophy of Wittgenstein's earlier period, that of the *Tractatus Logico-Philosophicus.*

The Atomistic Ontology of the Tractatus Logico-Philosophicus

One cannot grasp the *Philosophical Investigations* without a thoroughgoing familiarity with the *Tractatus.* Not only is there a certain continuity between the *Tractatus* and the *Philosophical Investigations,* but even more importantly the opinions discussed, attacked and refuted in the *Philosophical Investigations* are, with some exceptions, exactly those expounded by the younger Wittgenstein in the *Tractatus.*[1]

The argumentation of the *Tractatus* is closely connected with not only its contents, but also its structure.[2] The point of departure for a reading of the *Tractatus* is the proposition which Wittgenstein puts forth in the Preface: "That which can be said, can be said clearly." In other words, the *Tractatus assumes* that human language is meaningful. The fundamental thesis of the *Tractatus* is that a proposition is meaningful *only if* its meaning has been fully determined. A reading of the work should thus begin with Thesis.[3] Everything which comes before and after is an articulation of the presuppositions that one must *necessarily* make if the proposition is to have a determinate significance.[3] These necessary conditions for the possibility of a proposition's determinate significance include:

    a) The foundations of language are the 'atomic propositions', which are not at all dependent upon one another and are joined solely by means of external or extrinsic relations in an *extensional logic*.

    b) Assuming a realistic interpretation of language, language then has a refigurative function with respect to reality: the proposition must be a *picture* of a fact.

    c) So as to guarantee this refigurative function to the atomic propositions, which are the foundation of the significance of speech, reality must be composed of 'atomic *facts*', that are themselves the conjunctions of *simple objects*. In other words one presupposes an *atomistic ontology*.

    Wittgenstein never gives an example of these propositions or of these atomic facts: they are not empirical data but are as it were a "transcendental condition" for the possibility of making a significant proposition, and they form part of *that which cannot be said but which shows itself*.

    The doctrine of "that which cannot be said but which shows itself" is essential to the *Tractatus*. It applies not only to Wittgenstein's famous 'mystical' (6.522), to values and ethics (6.43), and the 'transcendental subject' (5.62-5.641), but to the whole primordial, elemental structure of reality and of language itself (3.22-3.23, 3.262), to the structure of the logical picture and of the proposition, the form of the refiguration, the logical form (4.022, 4.121), the internal and formal relations, the formal concepts (4.122-4.126), and even to the meaning and truth of the singular picture of the singular proposition, and to the very existence of the elementary propositions (5.5562-5.5571). This distinction between that which can be spoken, and that which cannot be spoken but which show, revives a central theme of transcendental philosophy: this corresponds to the Kantian division between the *object of the intelligence* ("Gegenstand der Verstandserkenntnis), i.e., the domain of the 'pure reason' on the one hand, and the *idea of the reason*, i.e., the domain of the 'practical reason', on the other. In the *Tractatus* this latter in fact comprehends the ultimate structure of the universe, the transcendental subject, ethics and the beyond.

In recent years the resurgence of interest in the relations between logic and ontology has brought a renewed attention to the *Tractatus*. But quite apart from this, the *Tractatus'* speculations on linguistic analysis, logic, ontology, and epistemology have secured it the reputation of a masterwork of analysis.

For an analysis of *religious* language the approach expounded in the *Tractatus* can be employed in the sense of a negative and apophatic theology: the specific significance of religious language *cannot be said but rather shows itself.* This echoes an ancient theme in both philosophy and theology, very evident in the whole of the neoplatonic movement. One must however take pains not to reduce *all that shows but cannot be stated* to the 'mystical' and then that to 'God'. In any case one needs to respect the 'elucidations' ("Erläuterungen") which Wittgenstein continually made in the *Tractatus*.[4] And obviously an ontology which is exclusively atomistic is unacceptable — and Wittgenstein himself, precisely by virtue of the doctrine of *that which cannot be said but which rather shows itself,* does not propose it. For our own inquiry however the *Philosophical Investigations* of Wittgenstein's second period are more significant.

The Philosophical Investigations

The philosophy which emerges in this later period is profoundly and deliberately nonsystematic, even anti-systematic, to such a degree that it is erroneous to speak, for example, of a 'philosophy of language games'. Thus the following observations do not in any way constitute the central 'theses' of the philosophy of Wittgenstein's latter period. They serve solely as points of orientation.

The *meaning* of linguistic expressions does not consist in their being names of real things, or of sense impressions, or of mental images, or of ideas or of contents or of anything.[5] "Naming' is a special linguistic game, often used as a preparation for the use of words within a determined context according to their customary function as, for example, is the case when teaching words to children. The 'ostensive definition',[6] so important to Bertrand Russell, can neither guarantee nor impart a foundation for speech. The ostensive definition is not univocal and can be misunderstood.

More importantly, even to understand an ostensive definition, a certain prior linguistic competence must be assumed: to learn a word, whether by means of an ostensive definition or by any other means, I must at the same time learn how to *use* the word later. This is to say that for any given word a place in the context of speech must already exist where it can be situated.[7] To say that words are signs all of which have a meaning is not to say very much, given that the very word 'meaning' can be used in a number of senses. Linguistic expressions have 'meaning' and are 'significative' in many different ways inasmuch as they have many and varied functions. This functional diversity of linguistic expressions is particularly apparent in the fact that we use them in diverse language games.

Unquestionably the concept of 'language games' is central to the later Wittgenstein's thought — which is not to say that Wittgenstein elaborated a 'theory of language games'. Rather, what is intended is an *analogy* between the term 'language' and the term 'game'. Through this analogy he wants to insist on the following points:

As is the case with playing, speaking is an *activity*. *Speaking is moreover a complex activity* that unites diverse elements, both linguistic and non- linguistic. Speaking, which is to say, using language, is a multiform activity, in a way analogous to the multiformity of that which we call 'playing', and as a multiform activity it is not reducible to some 'common essence' of speech. Moreover it is an activity intrinsically subject to public rules, which are more or less rigid according to the type and object of a given linguistic game. One must be aware however that for Wittgenstein, 'following a rule' is something which is *public and institutional,* and does not consist in feeling oneself directed or led by a rule. The significance of any single expression depends on its relation with other elements in the same linguistic game and thus on the *logic*, or on the 'grammar',[8] specific to the linguistic game in question. In addition, a number of language games pertain to a certain "form of life",[9] whereas speaking, i.e., using language in general, comprises part of the 'natural human story'.[10] The term 'linguistic game' refers both to the totality of speech and to singular 'games'. Wittgenstein considers speech as an integral part of the total picture of human behavior.[11] 'Private language', in the sense of expressions whose significance are wholly private, is non-sense.

Meaning. "The significance of a word is its use in language" runs the well-known dictum of Wittgenstein. But here too we need to take care to be precise, for this dictum is not a *definition* of meaning, but a functional description and analogy, given that "the use" can be most varied. Moreover, the *use* of which Wittgenstein is speaking is the *institutional* use which the word possesses in speech, not the personal use which one may make of it. Meaning is never something psychological and private, but always a reality which is public, social and cultural. Also, the exception of which Wittgenstein speaks in this context[12] refers to the fact that the words 'meaning' and 'significance' have various meanings. (For example, sometimes 'meaning' means 'importance'.)

In contrast with the philosophical position of the *Tractatus*, the *Philosophical Investigations* abandons the idea of certain 'ultimate elements' of language that would be intrinsically simple, i.e., not susceptible of further analysis and to which all linguistic expressions could be reduced by means of the appropriate analysis. For the later Wittgenstein not only the words 'simple', 'compound', but also 'identical' and 'diverse', have no absolute meaning but a meaning which varies according to the context of their appearance in various language games.

One uses the same word in speaking of various things not because all these things have a common essence or certain definable common characteristics, but rather because there exists a certain 'family resemblance' among the things[13]. We find no fixed limits separating diverse concepts; the borders of a concept is rather a question of use. It follows that questions of essence then are questions of grammar.[14] That which is considered as 'essence' depends upon the special logic of the linguistic game to which the concept in question appertains. Note that this does not negate the possibility that for the *specific* use of a word in a determinate language game, the use of the word – its content – becomes more rigorously fixed.

It follows then that the various concepts we humans employ are not the results of individual abstraction operations, but rather we acquire them in learning a language. The *intellectual* aspect of the formation of concepts consists in the intelligent appropriation of them which is demanded in order to learn a language. As a consequence all our everyday concepts are *analogies*. Only technical locutions which are part of a scientific terminology approach a certain univocality.

All this notwithstanding, Wittgenstein is no simple nominalist; the use of a word has reasons which are both objective and actual. However he is certainly no longer the ultrarealist of the *Tractatus*. Psychological vocabulary is worth special attention. The words which refer to human mental states, such as 'to feel pain', 'to want', 'to think', 'to understand', and so on, have meaning not insofar as they refer to an activity, to an event, or to a psychic state (i.e., something private and interior to consciousness), nor insofar as they refer to an external, observable behavior; the mentalist explanation of the Cartesians is as inaccurate as the comportmentalist explanation of the behaviorists. The psychological concept of pain, for example, is *one* but it is *asymmetrical:* its grammar for the first-person present indicative is different from its grammar in the other forms ("He feels pain" but also different from the first-person past tense: "I felt pain"). In the first instance ("I feel pain") the grammar is similar to that of the sheer expressions "Ow", "Ouch" — there are no criteria possible here; it makes no sense if one says: "I am certain that I am in pain", or " I'm probably in pain." (Though of course it is possible to tell a lie and to sham it.) In the other cases however there are criteria, and there exists the possibility of error, as well as the possibilities of doubt and of certainty. The concept however is *single*; such a concept is acquired and used – it has meaning – as a single concept though with asymmetrical use – not as two distinct concepts. The importance of Wittgenstein's observations here for an elaboration of a philosophical anthropology are apparent, but we must leave them aside.

The method. The method employed in the *Philosophical Investigations* is still that of linguistic analysis but with important differences. The method is no longer reductive as in the *Tractatus*, but descriptive, expository. He puts forth a theory of *logical function,* not of psychological function, a 'depth grammar' of various language games, not that of language in general.

In this, his method is not one of putting forth an argument, whether causal, physical, psychological, metaphysical, still less that of an inquiry into the existential determinations of speech or human communication. Nor is his method explicative in the way a scientific method attempts to explain facts or phenomena. Wittgenstein rigorously distinguishes philosophy from science and rejects any ideal 'scientific philosophy'. Linguistic analysis is concerned solely with meaning.

Considered *positively,* the method of the *Philosophical Investigations* is analytic; in his reflection on the multiform reality of speech he delibrately avoids generalized considerations. He describes various language games, indicating some similarities among them but emphasizing the differences.[15] Such a way of doing philosophy does indeed lend itself to a global and synthetic vision, but in this case that certainly does not entail a system to which everything can be reduced and from which all can be deduced; rather what we have here is an image of an ancient city in which one has learned to find the streets with ease. Wittgenstein never draws conclusions from nor abstracts a 'Summa' from his analyses; he does not, for example, pull together the various ways in which language functions in an attempt to make a statement about human nature. His method doesn't *permit* such an enterprise. For Wittgenstein the existence of a linguistic game is something ultimate, about which it makes no sense to ask *why.*

The point of the later Wittgenstein's linguistic analysis is primarily therapeutic-critical, not only against the sterile generalizations and one-sided nature of philosophy, but even more against the spontaneous errors inspired by the superficial grammar of our language. In reply to the question, What is the intention of your philosophy?, Wittgenstein said, "To show the fly the way out of the fly bottle."[16]

The ultimate utility of the linguistic analysis of the *Philosophical Investigations* does not end here, however. Its great contribution is clarificatory, bringing to light the way in which language games actually function, the relationships among them, and the illimited variety of speech.

If one wishes to elaborate a specific logic for a linguistic game, one must first compare the use of the linguistic expressions in this game with their use in other, similar games, indicating however the *differences.* In a *second* move, one must *look* in other language games for usages similar to those which, in the original case under analysis, seemed at first glance unique and simple. Thirdly, between the usage in the case under analysis and the other *different* uses, one must search for intermediate cases, even inventing them,[17] to create a continuum of these 'family resemblances'.

Now what are the characteristics of Wittgenstein's logical-linguistic method which make it useful for an analysis of Christian discourse about God?

1) The method of the *Philosophical Investigations* is a philosophical method. The method of linguistic analysis is neither philological nor sociological nor psychological. The question posed by Wittgenstein is a philosophical question: how is it that a linguistic expression has a *meaning?* How is the activity in which human beings engage when speaking, understood? This method is *not* a method specific to positive theology, which is to say, it is not an exegetical method of immediate usefulness in the interpretation of Sacred Scripture or of official documents of the Magisterium. Nor is it a method of speculative theology insofar as its function is neither one of hermeneutics nor of synthesis.

2) The method of the *Philosophical Investigations* is a descriptive method. This is to say that the method of linguistic analysis makes no claims to being *normative*. We observe how people speak, how they use their words, what meaning is had by that which they say. We cannot prescribe how they ought to speak, ought to use their words, or what meaning *should* be had by that which they say, according to a previously conceived norm. Precisely for this reason the method of Wittgenstein is not reductive. If the language is used in a determinate manner, i.e., if it has a determinate significance for those who use it, then this is simply to be accepted as a matter of fact, as a given. This is *not* the same as saying that all which is said is *true*, nor that the using of speech in this determinate manner is useful, advisable or necessary.[18]

For the Wittgenstein of the *Philosophical Investigations* it is *not legitimate* to say: "Such and such a linguistic expression cannot have this meaning, because the *language* cannot have such a meaning; thus the 'true' significance of certain linguistic expressions must be some other" — e.g., empirical, social, economic, political or simply poetic, mythical, etc. — that is, the 'true significance' must be one of the meanings which are *admitted* in virtue of a philosophical, religious or other position taken up *a priori*.

(3) The method of the *Philosophical Investigations* is an

analytical method. It serves only to arrive at syntheses whose scope is relatively limited and specific; it makes no attempt to reach a global systematization in which everything — world, human existence, history, or even simply language — is embraced by means of one grand perception.[19] Wittgenstein was on guard against any such attempts.

Undoubted y, the method does serve to elaborate partial syntheses, and is not confined to pure observation and analysis of single instances. Wittgenstein wanted to elaborate the special logic of *various* language *games*. But one does not achieve this through a perception of the essence of the respective games, nor by means of a simple abstraction of the general concept in a certain number of singular concrete cases. One needs instead to analyze single examples, comparing them, confronting examples of this game with examples from other similar games, and bringing to the fore in this way the *similarities and dissimilarities*. What is thus attained is not a perception of a fixed and stable essence, but something similar to the rules of a game that one can continue to play in common.

In a certain way the method does yield a global vision — not in the sense of a 'mother idea' – some generative concept, like a law of formation in mathematics (ax–by=c),[20] but in the sense of a map, or better: the 'global vision' of a city possessed by one who has lived there for years. Thus the method can serve as a preparation for new knowledge, perceptions and innovations. It can yield a rather precise picture — precise because detailed and, even more: nuanced, "analogical", one might say — of the relational 'sets' which are speech, science, knowledge, and also theology and the Christian faith.

4) The method of the *Philosophical Investigations* is a therapeutic method. When one begins to reflect upon language, the seeming immediacy of its structure can be delusive. Wittgenstein named this deceptive immediacy its 'superficial grammar'. This can especially happen when one transposes a speech form from its original context to a different context, as for example: when everyday language, or biblical language or the language employed in evangelization is brought into philosophy or theology. Problems then appear which in actuality do not exist. It is thus essential to dissipate these problems by demonstrating the real functioning of these linguistic expressions in their 'natural environment', which is not

philosophical and not theological — that is, in the respective language games to which they originally belong.[21]

This kind of philosophical and theological problem is quite frequent. Often we encounter it in the guise of a difficulty of comprehension or communication. The 'solution' consists not so much in argumentation with respect to the truth or falsehood of the given statements but in a clarification of the meaning of the linguistic expressions. Certain apparent problems dissolve when it is demonstrated that they simply do not apply. In this sense Wittgensteinian analysis has a therapeutic scope, inasmuch as it throws into relief *how* various speech forms are *really* used. It is 'therapeutic critique' not so much of language itself as of the spontaneous and uncritical acceptance of language which can prove very misleading. To this end Wittgenstein rigorously distinguishes between *actual* problems and logical/linguistical/grammatical problems.

Uses and limitations of the method. Generally speaking, one can borrow the analytical method of the *Philosophical Investigations* as the *first move* in any philosophical or theological undertaking, and often even for enterprises which are apparently scientific. At the same time it is obvious that this method remains one philosophical method among other philosophical methods which continue to be indispensible. Not all philosophical problems can be resolved or even handled by linguistic analysis, and not all can be 'cured' as if they were just so many maladies. It remains legitimate and necessary to do philosophy in ways other than those followed by Wittgenstein, to do things that philosophers have been doing for almost 2500 years with very different methods: the phenomenological method which seeks the structural unity of conscious human life in the world; the transcendental method which seeks the conditions of possibility of experience; the traditional metaphysical method which analyzes reality in analogical principles such as the principle of non-contradiction. However, linguistic analysis as Wittgenstein proposes it can well constitute not only a first pass, but also a continual test of meaningfulness, without which one falls all too easily into pseudo-problems.

In all this, but especially in the context of religious Christian discourse, the distinction between actual problems and other, logical-grammatical problems — a distinction so dear to Wittgenstein — must not be considered absolute and satisfying in all respects.

II. THE PHENOMENOLOGICAL 'REDUCTION': EDMUND HUSSERL 1859-1937

The phenom. nological method of Edmund Husserl has been often adopted, even if in a synthetical way, and for some time has found interest and application also in the theological sphere Thus our exposition here can be briefer.

Husserl's philosophy has a mathematical origin. He originally studied mathematics and quickly became engrossed in the conflict between the psychologists who sought to give a psychological foundation to the fundamental concepts of mathematics and the formalists who renounced any foundation, philosophical, psychological or otherwise, considering mathematics purely formal. In his first book, *On the Concept of Number,* the problem for Husserl is the mathematical 'one' as the fundamental concept not only for all of mathematics, but even for simple counting. This concept of *'one'* has no meaning if not that of not being the *'other'* – settting aside for a moment the question of any additional differences. The reduction of number to psychic process related to simple counting, inspired by the Brentano's notion of genetic reconstruction, leads Husserl to the concept of the pure 'something', without any differentiating qualification, as the foundation of the 'one'. And this concept of 'something'; would emerge from the unifying psychological act of identifying something as a one.

Husserl later abandoned the attempt at *genetic* reconstruction, whether of the fundamental concepts of mathematics or of any objectival content of consciousness. The horizons of Husserl's philosophical reflection became universal and all-inclusive. The center of his attention became the content, which is to say, the datum of consciousness in its pure objectivity ("Die Sachen selbst"). In the first part of his *Logical Investigations* Husserl poses the problem of the meaningfulness of signs — linguistic now as well as mathematical — and he confronts this problem by 'bracketing off' both the communicative moment and the sign's naturalistic reference. Husserl is seeking the pure reality of the 'logical', which he calls the 'essence' ("Wesen") — *the reality of the pure phenomenon as such,* as it presents itself to consciousness. This 'Wesen', the 'essence', is a *unity* which is no longer a simple 'something', but rather a unity of sense — it includes the perceiver; it is the reality of logic because logic as such already implies relational structures. At the same time, it is a 'phenomenon', describable as it presents itself, in a form, to consciousness. One refrains then from any *interpretative* identification of it, whether with the natural reality of things or with the reality of psychic acts. For this reason Husserl calls not only his method but his whole philosophy 'phenomenology'.

Immediately the problem of method thrusts itself forward. *How* does one arrive at and grasp this 'phenomenon' in its objectival purity? In the *Logical Investigations* Husserl uses the term 'abstraction', though not in the Lockean sense of simply putting aside concrete, particular and sensible differences – abstracting from them. Husserl, on the other hand, intends abstraction rather as a 'bracketing off' or 'switching off' ("Ausschalten") of that which he calls the natural attitude ("die natürliche Einstellung") – an attitude which leads us to consider a datum of consciousness either as a natural physical reality or as an event in the psychological development of the mind. Husserl wants thus to concentrate on the pure presence of content, i.e., on the phenomenon. This phenomenon is, of course, a content of consciousness; however, what counts is not the content of consciousness as such but the phenomenon in itself. At the same time Husserl continues to say with Brentano that the consciousness is *intentional,* that is, it is a consciousness of something; it is 'cogitatio' in which "ego cogitatio cogitatum qua cogitatum."

The Mature Phenomenology of the "Ideas on a Pure Phenomenology"[22]

In the "Ideas", Husserl deepens his phenomenology. The center of his attention is clearly the content of consciousness, now characterized as "that originarily and absolutely lived", anterior to any predication with factual interpretative references. The term used for this 'content' is first *'noema', 'Eidos',* and then later *'essence'* ("Wesen"), which is to be understood as the *intelligible structure* of the contents of consciousness (and not in the Aristotlean-thomistic sense of an ontological element constitutive of the finite singular being).

Husserl's phenomenological method continues to be refined and in a certain way takes a turn towards a *subjective pole*. If in fact the datum of consciousness must be purely objective, one must pass beyond the abstraction from the sensible and the particular. One must 'put in parentheses' the *double* existence of the datum: its psychological existence in me, and its realistic existence in itself, since both are contingent. "Bracketing off" or "switching off" ("Ausschalten") and "putting into parentheses" thus receive a new significance as the key word becomes *"epochè"*[23] – epochè not only from the act and from the subject, i.e., from my experience, but also from its concrete existence. With this Husserl's philosophical reflection takes a turn towards the subjective pole. Of interest now is not only the noema but also the noesis, which is to say, the *diverse* relationships of the subject, the *manifold* of his 'intentionality' towards the diverse kinds of content. The end of phenomenology remains, however, the same: the pure description of 'essence', i.e., of the unity of sense in every field of experience, from the most restricted to the most cosmic. But the experience is always essentially of an intentional character. Thus the 'rigorous science' towards which Husserl leans must have a twofold character: the description of the objective pole demands that we commit ourselves also to a description of the subjective pole.[24] Only thus, in the reference of the pure noesis to the pure noema does one come to the full 'adaequatio' of truth, and doubt ceases because one has all the evidence. The is the real sense of epochè.

The essential moment therefore in Husserl's method is the *'phenomenological reduction'*, by means of which one passes from the 'natural attachment', in which our attention is immediately and spontaneously drawn to the things in their natural existence, to the *'eidetic vision'*, i.e., to the vision of the logical forms constitutive of this world.

Husserl's chosen terminology has not only a Skeptic but also a Cartesian flavor (*epochè* —> methodological doubt). Not only does it therefore bring with it the problem of the subject as the counterpart of the ideal content, but also a turn towards the transcendental becomes explicit, precisely because the ideal content is not to be understood in a *Platonic* key. At the same time, this content is an *absolute* content, and thus the *pure* 'cogitatio' has need of a *pure* 'ego cogitans'; thus the subject cannot be other than *transcendental*. This level of the problem becomes clearly apparent in the Husserl's *"Ideas"*, and indeed many of the faithful disciples of the Master of Göttingen felt themselves betrayed by this 'transcendental turn' which seemed to be a return to Kant.

We must leave aside Husserl's last and ultimate exploration of a transcendental phenomenology for despite its importance it does not address our own interests here. We need now to examine the application of Husserl's method to religious discourse.

The Application of Husserl's Method to Religious Discourse

In the first place, Husserl's phenomenological method[25] deals with objects, or rather with *objectuality*. For Husserl himself that which remains important is the paradigm of number, the idea of meaning, and in general the *eidos*. But in the disciples of Husserl we encounter the 'community' ("Gemeinschaft"), the 'society' ("Gesellschaft"), the 'state' (Scheler and Stein) and also the 'sacred' (Rudolf Otto); we do not however encounter 'language' or 'religious language' as the focus of attention. On the other hand, Husserl himself, and even more so his disciples, undertook the analysis of diverse types of *intentionality* on the part of the subject (the 'noesis'), towards the 'noema', the content of consciousness. Thus in a second move the phenomenological method of Husserl can be applied (and has been so) to *intentional human actions* (Stein: empathy; Merleau-Ponty: sensibility; Ricoeur: will, etc.) Such intentional human actions would include, for example, "to believe", "to pray", "rite", "sacrifice", etc. This is obviously most important for a phenomenology of religion and especially for a phenomenology of the Christian *faith*, in which there is a strict correlation between content and act of faith.

Only in a third move does this method serve to determine a global reality such as 'society' (Scheler) or 'religion', and then it must be supported by results from the first and second levels of application of the phenomenological method.

In the use of the phenomenological method at the first two levels, one seeks to individuate an objective structural reality, distinguishing in its specificity from all others. This reality is neither individual nor collective, but simply objective. In a reductive act one then eliminates from this every singular and particular aspect, and also every dependence on the subject, whether individual or collective. For this very reason an application of the phenomenological method to problems of faith should lead neither to a psychologization nor to a sociologization of theology. At the same time however it precludes a *naturalistic realism* with regard to the contents of the Christian faith.

In the conte. t of this book the phenomenological method will serve us not so much to determine religious *language*, but rather the *objects* and *acts* specific to the Christian faith. We will employ it most fully in the last two chapters.

Methodological Pluralism

As distinct from linguistic analysis, the phenomenological method reduces a concrete diversity to a single unique structural essence, and does *not* seek to make the institutional rules of a game manifest. Moreover, this structural essence becomes determined as *unitary, not* as multiform, and it tends to distinguish precisely this essence from other similar ones.[26]

At this point one could justifiably ask why two methods so diverse could be used together in an analysis of Christian discourse about God. For quite some time I have been of the opinion that there is no such thing as *one* philosophical method; rather there are a plurality of methods which are to be used in philosophy: besides the logical-analytical and the phenomenological methods there are also the classical aristotelian-scholastic method, the transcendental method, etc., etc. One needs to have a variety of methods at one's disposal – not only in the various branches of philosophy but also for each particular philosophical problem.

Moreover the differences between Husserl's phenomenology and the linguistic analysis of the later Wittgenstein are not so great as may appear. In the latter part of the *Philosophical Investigations* one finds formulations very similar to Husserl's . And certain paragraphs on linguistic meaning in the *Logical Investigations* and in the *Ideas* resembles those of Wittgenstein. More importantly, however, the way in which the logic of a linguistic game is to be understood is not unlike the 'eidetic vision' of an 'essence'. Both require a labor of methodical preparation which is both long and difficult, but in the end 'comprehension' is achieved.

Both treat of the 'vision' of a whole, not reducible to its parts and not 'reconstructible' from them.

Common to both phenomenology and linguistic analysis is also their object, which is generally if not exclusively: *meaning*. In this lies their common limitation as well: neither phenomenology nor linguistic analysis can offer *foundational* arguments. Both analyze what a moral duty is or what religious faith is, but with neither of the two methods can one *demonstrate* the existence of God or the bindingness of a given moral imperative. Both the datum of consciousness and the linguistic game with its rules are, as it were, *ultimate*, and in this inheres their fatal attractiveness today. For if *all* of philosophy is exclusively phenomenology or linguistic analysis or both together, then we lose metaphysics, and with that we lose any attempt at an *ultimate foundation*. Neither Husserl nor Wittgenstein suggest this, but certain of their distant followers do.

NOTES

1. Cfr. *Philosophical Investigations*, intro. and no. 46.

2. The *Tractatus* is arranged by means of a decimal system from 1.000 to 7. See PG. 27 excerpts from tractatus.

3. The use of Kantian language here is deliberate and the reasons for its use will shortly become clear.

4. Cfr. for example, *Tractatus* 6.54.

5. Cfr. PU 1, 5, 26, 27, 40, 361.

6. An 'ostensive definition' refers to the presentation of a word by means of a verbal indicator ("this"), or a non-verbal indicator (pointing with the finger, etc.), while stating either a singular name ("This is Napoleon") or a general name ("This is a horse").

7. Cfr. PU 13,31,33,38.

8. Wittgenstein employs these two terms in an almost identical way.

9. Cfr. PU 19,21,241.

10. Cfr. PU 7.

11. The distinction between vaious language games is not absolute. According to the aspect under consideration, various language games can be considered as distinct *or* as one single unique game.

12. PU 43: "For the great number of cases, even if not for all cases, the word 'meaning' can be defined thusly: The meaning of a word is its use in the language."

13. Aristotle, in Book IV of the *Metaphysics*, speaks of a variety of similar terms as 'pollachos legontai'. Aquinas translates this as 'multipliciter dicuntur'.

14. Cfr. PU 371. "The essence is expressed in the grammar." Cfr. also 1, 46,65,92,97,113,116.

15. "I will teach you differences", he announced to his classes.

16. See: Garth Hallett, "The Bottle and The Fly," *Thought*, 46 (1971), 83-104.

17. These singular linguistic games of which Wittgenstein treats are either *natural and realistic* or simplified or even *invented, impossible* for human beings as we know them and therefore *absurd*. We see then that the philosophical method of the later Wittgenstein is not purely descriptive, and in a certain sense is similar to the method of phenomenology.

18. Here lies an essential difference between the method of linguistic analysis and that of phenomenology and existential analysis, which insists on the diverse authenticity and existential value of certain ways of speaking.

19. Here is another fundamental difference between the method of Wittgenstein and that of phenomenology and existential analysis.

20. Descartes' 'clear and distinct ideas' are recalled here.

21. Biblical exegesis accomplishes something similar when it seeks to identify the *Sitz im Leben* of Gospel passages.

22. The name phenomenology is not taken so much form the Kantian distinction between "phenomenon" and "numenon" as from the "Phenomenology of the Spirit" of Hegel, and even more from the ancient astronomy that speaks of "sozein ta fainomena".

23. The term *epochè* is borrowed from the vocabulary of the ancient Greek sceptics, where it meant: to abstain from any affirmation so as to avoid the danger of falling into error. In Husserl, however, the meaning of epochè is to put into parentheses both the natural existence and the psychological existence. The function of the epochè is *methodological*. In this, Husserl comes quite close to the methodological doubt of Descartes.

24. This commitment to the subjective pole is quite distinct however from the psychologism with which Husserl began his career and which he was later to radically criticize).

25. There are other methods which go by the name 'phenomenological', but we will be using Hussserl's, and using it rigorously insofar as that is possible.

26. In all this one can note Husserl's affinity not only with Plato, but also with the 'clear and distinct ideas' of Descartes.

CHAPTER THREE

THE CONCEPT OF RELIGIOUS LANGUAGE

It is not possible to analyze the religious speech form 'in general', as we already noted above, because religious discourse exists only as Christian discourse, Islamic discourse, Buddhist discourse, etc.

Now however we arrive at a different problem. *How* is religious discourse, and especially Catholic discourse, different from other, non-religious speech forms? More precisely, how are we to distinguish *the way in which Christians speak,* that is, the way in which they employ language in the context of their faith, from the way they speak outside of the religious context?

To clarify this problem we will use the analytical method of Wittgenstein, as set forth in the preceding chapter. The first question we need to answer is: does there exist a Christian religious discourse *alongside of* common speech? The response to this question is in the negative!

There Does Not Exist a Christian Language To One Side of Ordinary Language

If, on the level of 'superficial grammar',[1] we compare the way in which Christians employ language in the context of their faith with the way in which they speak outside of this context, we do not note real differences. For the most part, any concrete religious language — in our case, Christian religious language — does not differ from the non-religious, non-Christian speech forms which human beings, Christians included, commonly speak. Christian religious speech, and other religious speech forms as well, does not differ from ordinary non-religious discourse as spoken by these same Christians or by adherents of the other religions. As we shall see, this is rather important, but it does not however dispense us from a further analysis at the level of 'deep grammar', which will reveal genuine differences between *the use* of religious language and non-religious language.

Religious Language Does Not Differ from Ordinary Language as Regards Its Vocabulary

The *words* used in a Christian religious context are the same that one uses in daily speech: 'father', 'grace', pardon', etc., etc.

The specific *technical terms* of the language of faith that are used in Christiaı discourse are relatively rare and not indispensable, because they are explainable by means of common terms. Examples of such technical terms would be: 'prayer', 'salvation', 'redemption', etc. A goodly number of these terms specific to Christian discourse are of a practical and juridical nature, for example: 'church', 'parish', 'chalice', 'bishop', etc., and in a number of cases are taken from other languages, notably Latin and Greek.

Theology, on the other hand, as the reflective science of faith — or as Wittgenstein would say, the *grammar of the language of faith*[2] — has, as does every science, a number of special terms: 'transubstantiation', 'circumincession', 'trinitarian', etc.

Religious Language Does Not Differ from Ordinary Language as Regards Its Grammar

The grammar which Christians employ, even when doing theology, is simply that of the language which they speak — Greek, Latin, Italian, English, etc. It is not true that religious discourse is grammatically 'strange'.[3] An error in English grammar is an error even when found in a book of theology.

Religious Language Does Not Differ from Ordinary Language as regards Its Style

In a religious context, also and especially in a specifically Christian context, one can use *all* or almost all of the styles that are used in any other context: poetical or prosaic; elevated or everyday or banal; infantile, adolescent or adult; learned or simple; correct or poor.

Religious Language Does Not Differ from Ordinary Language as regards Its So-called Language Games

Wittgenstein, in his Philosophical Investigations, offers the following list of what he calls language games,[4] a list that is obviously incomplete and indeed *cannot* be completed:

> To command and to act according to a command.
> To describe an object according to it speech appearance
>   and dimension.
> To construct an object according to a description (design).
> To make hypotheses concerning a phenomenon.
> To elaborate a hypotheses and submit it to a test.
> To make up a story and read it.
> To recite in the theater.
> To sing in nursery rhymes.
> To solve riddles.
> To make a joke; to tell it.
> To resolve a problem of applied arithmetic.
> To translate from one language to another.
> To ask, thank, beg, greet, pray.[5]

Certainly not all language games can be 'played' in all situations, and therefore not all can be played in religious situations either. One such example from the above list would be "To represent the results of an experiment by means of tables and diagrams". But that fact in itself is not what makes up the special character of religious language. Moreover the overwhelming majority of the language games of everyday life are in fact played also in a Christian religious context. To be sure, in such cases there are specific nuances at work and sometimes even a special *name,* different than the name given when these games are played in a non-religious context: for example,: "to request - to pray"; "to declare a conviction - to make a profession of faith", etc.

"Religious Language"[6] *Does Not Differ from Non-Religious Language in the Way That German or French, for Example, Does from English*

A Christian Englishman does not speak *two* languages: English and 'Christian'. One does not translate from 'Christian' into English, just as one does not translate from scientific language into English. At the same time, there is no translating from religious language into empirical or 'lay' language, nor from 'Christian language' into common language.

Religious Language Does Not Differ from Non-Religious in the Way That a Dialect Differs from the Official, Accepted Language

Religious Language Does Not Differ from Non-Religious in the Same Way That the Jargon of a Particular Group Differs from Other Types of Speech

There exist forms of discourse peculiar to guilds, social groups, age groups, etc. All of these differences are found within a religious, Christian, Catholic use of language as well. A Catholic youth group develops its own group language. Indeed every church movement has its jargon. The great and varied forms of Christian spirituality have all developed their own terminology. These speech forms too must be learned, and their diversity can create problems.

The way of using language in the context of a particular religion (and also within a particular movement), with words of special significance (*grace, Eucharist, penance*) and with a predilection for certain expressions (*way, path, exodus*) serve *also* as a means of identifying the group and the individual within the group. Precisely for this reason this specific way of speaking is acquired by means of a *process of linguistic socialization.*

Religious Language Does Not Differ from Non-Religious in the Same Way That a Technical/ Scientific Language Differs from Common Language

In addition to Christian-Catholic discourse exists also the discourse of theology, which is often a technical language. Even practicing believers, with a good religious formation, do not generally possess a linguistic competence in this special language — notwithstanding that they are in possession of a true *common* linguistic competence in the context of their faith.

THERE IS A SPECIAL WAY OF USING LANGUAGE IN A RELIGIOUS CONTEXT

The above notwithstanding, it is a fact that the *way* of speaking in a religious context is a specific way, different from the way of speaking in a non-religious context. This is seen in the *difficulty* in understanding the special linguistic usage within the various religions, even within Christianity and among the diverse Christian denominations, as for example, between Catholics and Evangelicals. Even a person who genuinely possesses full linguistic competence in his or her given language can *not understand* this faith-specific way of speaking, especially today. If he lives in a culture which has not been determined by Christianity, then he will surely either misunderstand or simply ignore the Christian way of speaking about God. Therefore one has to *learn, acquire* religious linguistic usage. Often this occurs in a normal process of religious socialization. In the case of Catholics the catechism and the preparation for the sacraments of "Christian Initiation" *also* serve this function. Notwithstanding, even among Catholics there is too often a lack of *reflective* competence with respect to the religious language they use, with the consequence of not infrequent misunderstandings, and even superstitions.

CONCLUSION

1. Not only the term 'language' but also 'religious language' are *analogous* terms, sometimes even 'equivocal' perhaps, but in no case univocal.

2. Religious discourse stands in strict relation to common everyday discourse. In this regard the structure of Christian religious language *mirrors* the relation between *faith and life* and between *grace and nature,* according to Aquinas' statement: "Gratia supponit et elevat naturam."

3. The differences found between the Christian religious usage and other uses of speech are to be determined positively:

a) because of the *central role* played by the word "God" or its equivalents;[7]

b) because of the *special significance* that all other expressions acquire when use in reference, direct or indirect, to "God".

NOTES

1. Wittgenstein, PU 664: In the use of a word one can distinguish a 'superficial grammar' ("Oberflächengrammatik") from a 'deep grammar' ("Tiefengrammatik"). That which expresses itself immediately in us, with the use of a word, is the way it is employed in the *construction of a proposition* ("im Satzbau") – that aspect of its use which, so to speak, we grasp with the ear.

2. Cfr. PU 373.

3. Cfr. J.T. Ramsey, *Religious Language on an Empirical Basis* (London: SCM, 1967).

4. Cfr. PU 83, passim.

5. PU 23.

6. It would be preferable to say "the way of speaking in a religious context", but for simplicity we will continue to say, "religious language".

7. See chapter 4.

PART II

THE LOGIC OF CHRISTIAN DISCOURSE
ABOUT GOD

CHAPTER FOUR

THE ROLE, USE AND SIGNIFICANCE OF THE WORD "GOD"

At the conclusion of the preceding chapter we indicated the *centrality* of the word "God" with respect to religious linguistic usage. Eliminating the word "God" from religious language *alters the significance* of all other expressions. These then lose their meaning, simply retaining perhaps a psychological, sociological, political, or poetical significance. All other expressions, even if not the sum total of them, can be eliminated or changed *without* causing the religious significance of discourse to disappear. Perhaps the *type* of religion would change: If Christ were eliminated from Christian discourse, such discourse would no longer be a *Christian* discourse, but it could be still a Jewish discourse.

All the other expressions, not only of Christian discourse but of *any* religious discourse, possess a significance *specifically* religious by means of their relation, direct or indirect, to the word "God".[1]

With respect to *Christian* discourse about God, the word "Jesus", which linguistically is a proper name, has a similar centrality and systematically substitutes for the word "God" in many contexts. The most patent example is the "Holy, Holy, Holy" sung during the Eucharistic Liturgy. In the Book of the Apocalypse, from which the liturgy has taken it, it is proclaimed of Jesus, but in Isaiah it refers to Jaweh.[2] One quickly observes however that the substitution of the word "God" with the proper name "Jesus" is not possible in all contexts. The Christian doctrine of the "Trinity" develops linguistically, precisely out of the fact of insubstitutibility, when for example, Jesus himself addresses the Father. An explicit reflection on this subject from a logical/linguistic viewpoint constitute be found in the elaboration of the "communicatio idiomatum" by the Fathers of the Church.[3]

THE USE AND MEANING OF THE WORD "GOD" IN CHRISTIAN DISCOURSE

The function of the word "God" in Christian religious discourse is in many respects similar to that of a *proper name;* this is *not* however to say that for this reason the word "God" is actually to be considered as one proper name among other proper names.

According to certain logical-linguistic theories words are all *names,* either proper names of particular individuals, or common, general names of a *class* of individuals.[4] The distinction between proper names and *qualities* can be considered in this light, since 'qualities' — for example, 'red', 'heavy' — would be names common to a *class* of individuals. In such a case proper names are "indicators" and serve only to *indicate* a single object, but have no *informative* content which could tell us what kind of individual this is. That, on the other hand, is the function of "common names", whose content is informative inasmuch as they describe an object by *classifying* it.

Now if the word "God" were a proper name in this sense, it would have no informative content. In consequence one could use the word "God" only to speak *to God,* that is, to pray, but it would not serve to tell us *who God is.*

Given then that God is unique, which is to say, absolutely singular, we cannot attribute to Him other *common* or *general* names insofar as He cannot be 'classed' – He is not a member of a class of objects, together with other members. One could then speak *to* Him but never *about* Him, whether in catechesis, theology, preaching, or other contexts.

Is the Word "God" a Proper Name?

In the light of certain aspects of 'superficial grammar' the word "God" in Christian usage would seem to be a proper name: the word "God" is written with a capital letter as all other proper names. It is not used, except in rare instances, with an article ("The God"). Nor is it employed in the plural, or with an indeterminate article: "a God", unless with respect to a pagan divinity or in a negative form: "Apollo is not a true God."

On the other hand the word "God" is *translated* (Theos,

Deus, Dio, Gott, God) while other proper names are not translated, at lest after they cease being descriptions and become proper names ("Peter"="rock"). At the most, proper names become *transliterated* from one language to another, in conformance with phonetical, grammatical, and orthographical rules of the other language: Mediolanum=Milano=Mailand=Milan; Karl= Carlo=Karel=Charles.

What is a Proper Name? At this point we need to ask ourselves how the words we ordinarily call 'proper names' function within the usage of our language. The fundamental error of a linguistic analysis unilaterally determined by 'superficial grammar' and by formal logic consists in considering exclusively the *indicative function* of certain proper names within a singular proposition: "Socrates is mortal," whereas the words we generally call proper names are used not for one unique function but for a complex of overlapping functions.

The proper name is used to *address* a particular person;

The proper name is used to *speak about* a particular person to others;

The proper name is used to *identify* a particular person: "This is Mr. Smith";

The proper name is used to *call* a particular person: "Harry, come here."

The proper name is used to *introduce* an individual to others, allowing them to address him in turn: "This is Mr. Smith." "And I am Mary Jane Jones" — and there are still other possibilities with yet other purposes. Already in this brief exercise in analysis of the actual *usage* of proper names, conducted in the style of Wittgenstein, one sees just how reductive is the position of Russell and the others mentioned above.

A proper name serves *all* of these functions together, especially that of speaking *to* a person in his presence and of speaking *about* a person, often in his absence. One cannot correctly use a proper name if one doesn't know that this same name can be used for all the other functions enumerated above. This is true also when for cultural-linguistic reasons one uses a diversity of expressions in different contexts, for example: "The last president of the USSR", "The last Chairman of the Central Committee", "Comrade Gorbachov", "Mikhail". For a correct use in these cases it is

necessity that the reference of the various expressions always be
the same.

In certain situations a proper name can also serve to
communicate information. For example, I have already given some
information about Frank Smith, who is unknown to my hearers, and
afterwards I present him to them, saying: "This is Frank Smith". In
that case the *use of the proper name is informative,* though it
remains true the *mere* name "Frank Smith" does not give this
information.

Nonetheless it remains true that the word "God" as used by
Christians and by all those who believe in *one God* has something
important in common with proper names: they refer to a *unique*
object; at the same time, the *functions* of the word "God" within
Christian religious language are *multiple,* as with the functions of
proper names.

The Word "God" as an Expression Has a Unique Reference

Besides the word "God", there are other such linguistic
expressions which have a *unique* object. We need to look at them
briefly.

Proper names.   Proper names, as we have seen, are the
most noteworthy member of this group. There are times however
when the mere use of a proper name is not sufficient to guarantee
its function of identifying a *unique* object, but only creates equivocal
situations. At the university where I teach, for example, there are
two "professor Huber's, such that it is continually necessary to add
first names, if known, or descriptions, of which we shall shortly
speak, or employ other linguistic instruments, for example: numbers,
demonstrative pronouns, indicative gestures.

We need to add that one doesn't use proper names to refer
to *all singular objects.* Proper names are used only for persons,
for certain domestic animals and certain material objects, for cities
and countries, for stars, mountains and rivers, hurricanes, etc. When,
on the other hand, one refers to *other* singular objects, one uses
other linguistic instruments of unique reference.

Full Descriptions.   Describing a particular object by means of diverse characteristic, each of which is *common* to a class of objects, but which taken together belong to this particular object only, one arrives in fact at the identification of a unique object. How complex and extensive such a description should be is not a logical problem, but a practical one. A 'logically complete' description is an absurdity. The completeness which is both practical and *necessary* depends on the context and the situation, and cannot be determined a priori. It is sufficient to say, "Give me the yellow book" if among all the books in the room only one is yellow.

Singular Personal Pronouns. "I", "thou", "you", "he", "she", when concretely employed, have a unique reference. Their linguistic-grammatical function is that of substituting, in certain contexts, proper names. Thus they have come to be called "pronomi". If – as can happen in philosophy – they are used abstractly ("the I", "the Thou"), they then generally lose their identification function.

Numbers. The use of the *cardinal number 'one'* guarantees *singularity,* and thus a unique reference, but does not serve for purposes of identification because *every* singular thing is 'one'. For this reason one takes pains in logic to distinguish the singular proposition from the universal and particular propositions. *Ordinal Numbers* ("first", "second", "third", and so on) have a unique reference and serve to identify a unique object if they refer to a *determinate* class of objects, either explicitly or by way of a context or situation. This holds true also for the word "unique". And in certain branches of mathematics a *cardinal number*, in a way both absolute and abstract, can be a proper name of the respective number, or also of the respective abstract set: "the two", the "six", and so on.

The following linguistic expressions can refer to *a unique object* when they occur not by themselves but *together with other* linguistic expressions:

Demonstrative Pronouns. The most general of linguistic instruments, while at the same time fundamental for referring to a singular object and therefore the most concrete, is the use of the *demonstrative pronoun* together with the general name of a class:

"this dog", "this man". Already Aristotle identified this as the fundamental mode of speaking of *something determinate : "tode ti"*, "hoc aliquid", "this *such"*. From this way of speaking *about* reality, Aristotle arrived at the necessity of the idea of *"prote ousia"*, the 'primary substance" – the unique concrete reality, the *this* – which is not reducible to the *"deutera ousia"*, "the secondary substance", which is expressed with a universal term, a class name – the *such.*

Possessive Pronouns. In certain contexts the unique reference is guaranteed through the use of the possessive pronouns "my", "our", etc. — "my house", "your father". Also the determinate article "the", when used in an absolute sense, can function this way: *"the* father", *"the* house".

Titles and Names of Unique Functions. In certain contexts titles and names of functions, for example, "king", "lord", "father", but also "doctor", "professor", "pastor", and so on, have a unique reference: in this context and for a variety of reasons they exist only one at a time. These titles and names of functions may perhaps be qualified by the determinate article *"the* pastor", or better, with the possessive pronoun: *"my* father", *"our* king", *"our* rock", *"my* refuge". But at times the function is unique *per se:* "the King" — because there is no other.

The Singularity of the Word "God" in a Monotheistic Context

Also the word "God", as used in a monotheistic context, has a *unique reference,* and in this respect forms part of the group of words under consideration. For reasons then of "superficial grammar" the word "God" is indeed similar to proper names, of which we have spoken above. All pertain to the class of words with a unique reference. The similarities vary however according to the *various kinds* of the words which have a unique reference, listed above.

In this context certain similarities of the word "God" with other terms of unique reference are of special importance.

First of all, there are the terms used in Sacred Scriptures when they speak of God. There are the "titles of God" in the Old

Testament: "Lord", "King", "Shepherd", but also "The Holy One of Israel", and others; then there are also the "Christological titles" of Jesus which are, moreover, often taken from that same Old Testament: "the Christ", "the Messiah", "the Redeemer", "the Son of Man", "the Son of David", "the Son" (used absolutely), "the Son of God", "the Son of the Father", and others. Precisely in this context arises the theological-philosophical discussion on the "Divine Names", from Dionysius the Areopagite to Ockham: God has need of a name, because he is unique; but God does not have a name in the same way as do the persons of this world, who are to be distinguished from one another. God has many names, all of which however refer to *the Same*.[5] This discussion has been continued in Apologetics and in "Fundamental Theology" in the traditional section on "Christological Titles".

The linguistic usage of the Sacred Scriptures, particularly of the Old Testament, gave rise to a consideration of the use of *personal pronouns* for God. The Old Testament often avoids not only the word "Yahweh", particularly forbidden by the Second Commandment, but also alternative linguistic expressions, substituting the word "God" with a pronoun "He": "He has done marvels for us." The use of personal pronouns, especially the "Thou" with a capital letter, has a biblical foundation in prayer, especially in the psalms, but receives speculative elaboration in the modern philosopher-theologians of a personalistic orientation: Rosenzweig, Buber, Levinas and others. But historical precedents for the use of personal pronouns for God, at least as "I", are found already in Augustine, Descartes and Kant.

Of no small importance in this context is the fact that also the term 'universe' is a term of unique reference. Even in contemporary cosmology the term "the Universe" is a 'singularity'.[6] "Universe", as also "world", is a term of unique reference because it is a term which points to an unlimited totality or, as Kant would say, an Idea of the Pure Reason. Precisely for this reason the term "Universe" has a specific logical similarity with the term "God", which Cusanus pointed out[7] even before Kant.[8]

Conclusion

All that we have said in this chapter not only does not

constitute a 'definition' of the word "God", but still does not impart any *content* to the term. We have set forth the significance of the word "God" only in the sense of its central importance for Christian religious discourse and it *logical* function as a term of unique reference. In the next chapter we will take up the *contentual* significance of the term "God" by way of God's attributes and the special way of using them. We will return however to the "names" of God in the eighth and ninth chapters when we turn to a consideration of the various horizons of transcendental opening in human experience and thought, and how they come to center upon God or how they come to focus around God.

NOTES

1. See Chapter 5.

2. Cfr. Is. 6: 3, and Apoc. 4: 8. Out of this linguistic convergence one can make an argument for the divinity of Christ in Sacred Scripture.

3. See for example, Thomas Aquinas, *Lect. II* in 1Cor 2, and *Summa Th.Q.* 16a.4.

4. See for example, John Locke, *An Essay Concerning Human Understanding*, iii, 1-3; but also Carnap, *The Logical Syntax of Language* (London, 1951); and especially, Bertrand Russell, "The Philosophy of Logical Atomism," *The Monist*, 1918.

"Onoma" in Aristotle and its definition in *Peri hermeneias*, chapter 2, has a different meaning. Cfr. Also Petrus Hispanus, *Summulae logicales* (Venetiis, 1610), *Tractatus primus*, p. 17.

5. Cfr. Aquinas *S.T.I.* q.13 a.2-11. — Ockham, *S.L.* I,63; Quodlibet III q.2. — Suarez, *Disp.Met.* XXX sect. 6; *De divina substantia*, lib. I, chaps. 10-14.

6. Cfr. B. Kanitscheider, *Kosmologie* (Stuttgart, 1984) (with an extensive bibliography); S.W. Hawking, *Brief History of Time* (New York: Bantam, 1998), p. 72, passim.

7. Nicholas Cusanus, *De Docta Ignorantia*, II, 4, 112ss.

8. Kant, *Crituique of Pure Reason*, A 367-394: The Transcendental Dialectic: Book 1, "On the Concepts of the Pure Reason".

CHAPTER FIVE

THE LOGIC OF THE ATTRIBUTES OF GOD

The role and significance of the word "God" as Christians — and others — use it it cannot be explained by reflecting only on this one word. The word "God" is always used in a context, even if one is only exclaiming, "Oh God!". To determine then not only the meaning of what Christians say about God, but also to understand the meaning of the very word "God" we need to analyze *what is said about God,* that is, how are the diverse words of human speech used to speak about God.

To do this we will take up a discussion already alluded to in the preceding chapter — the very ancient discussion on the "Divine Names".

As with all words, even those terms of unique reference, the word "God" is not used in isolation but as a *subject* with logical-linguistic functions. Something is said *about* God, and is said in diverse ways, even when saying something *to* God, i.e., praying. We will take into special consideration *propositions* in which the term "God" functions primarily as subject; but what we shall say will be equally valid for inquiries, disputations, requests, etc., that contain the word "God". In all these ways of speaking about God, one uses, in various ways, other terms as *attributes,* connecting them with the term "God".

"Attribute" here is intended in a logical sense, that is, as any *predicate* (function) that can be united with the subject "God", as that subject has been determined in the preceding chapter.

Linguistically, the attributes, or predicates, of "God" can be:

nouns: "God is the universal King", "God is the father of all", "God is the Absolute";

Adjectives: "God is good", "God is one";

Verbs: "God loves us", "God has saved us", "God became man";

The reference to God can be immediate: "God is good", or indirect: "the goodness of God", or also "to ask God".

All these attributes can be used in *propositions,* either affirmative
or negative, or in disputations, questions, requests (prayers) and so
forth.

We generally distinguish attributes which are direct and concrete
— attributes of the *first degree:* "Father", "merciful" — from formal
attributes — attributes of the *second degree,* so called because
they implicate an explicit reflection on *the way in which* God is
spoken of: "transcendent", "one", "triune", etc. This distinction is
not wholly satisfactory however, as we shall see.

Both kinds of attributes may be either of a natural order: "just",
"transcendent"; or of a supernatural order: "Son", "Holy Spirit",
"triune". Obviously this distinction is not entirely satisfactory either.
It is in the *natural attributes of the first degree* that we see most
clearly the basic structure of the analogical passage from
significance of the *human* order to significance which refers to
God.

"NATURAL" ATTRIBUTES: THE "MODEL"

When we speak of God we necessarily use the words we already
know and which, within the tongue we speak, have a meaning –
that is, are used – without however the specific shading they acquire
when these same words are used as functions of the subject "God".[1]
This *non-religious significance* of a word constitutes the *model*
for it use in speaking about God.

"Model" here is intended in a sense very similar to the sense intended
by Ian T. Ramsey,[2] as *the commonly known, recognized meaning
of a word used in speech,*[3] which permits one to pass to a similar
but less common significance, not recognized by all.

For these attributes of God we must obviously use words *existing*
in human language. Not all human expressions can be used as
attributes of God, however, but only those that have certain
characteristics. The linguistic expressions which are used as
attributes of God must have:

   a *positive* connotation;
· a horizontally analogical meaning — that is, at the level of *human*
significance.

   gradations of significance already at the human level.

Let us now look more closely at these three 'musts.'4

Linguistic Expressions Used as Attributes of God Must Have a Positive Value

In order to be used as an attribute of God a linguistic expression must have a positive meaning, which is to say, it must express a *value*. This can be of the moral order ("just"), social order ("king", "shepherd"), or even economic ("rich"), among others. Non-positive expressions for God can be used only in the negative: "God is not *evil*", "God is not *dependent* on anything", etc.

One must however pay attention to the linguistic context, whether general or particular, that determines the *mutable* connotative value of the words: for example, the word "master"once had a positive value; now it has a negative value. In a situation where the children have been abandoned by their father, even the word "father" can have a negative connotation. The positive connotation is however always recoverable, and in the case of the word "father" it is necessary to recover it: "I too would like to have such a father!" Even an expression which is ordinarily negative can be given a positive value: "Christ humbled himself, and made himself obedient even unto death" "God died for us", etc.

Neutral expressions, such as "red", "heavy", "long", which do *not* have any valuation, cannot serve as attributes of God.

The exclusion of negatively-valued expressions is reflected in the moral prohibition against blasphemy. The exclusion of *neutral* expressions on the other hand, is reflected in the prohibition against magic and superstitions.

Linguistic Expressions Used as Attributes of God Must Have a Significance Which Is Analogical on the Ordinary — Horizontal — Semantic Level

Only expressions which can be used analogically in *non-religious* discourse can be used as attributes of God: "good", "one", "rich", as well as "father", "son", "spirit". This then precludes the use of technical — and thus univocal — terms which belong to specialized terminologies such as physics, economy, politics, informatics. It is however possible for a univocal technical term to acquire or reacquire analogical potential, as for example, "energy", "liberation". But it is also possible for a term to lose its analogical significance. One needs only to think of "Unmoved Mover".

A subsequent *vertically* analogical employment of a word through its *qualification*5 *toward the infinite,* must therefore presume the possibility of a 'horizontally' analogical use of the same word in a *non-religious* context. Indeed speech forms of faith presuppose and *guarantee* the multi-dimensionality of language and of human life against any scientific or political totalitarianism.6

Linguistic Expressions Used as Attributes of God Must Have a Graduated Significance at the Common Semantic Level

This is already implicit in the discussion above: for a term to be an attribute of God, it must be have a positive value-connotation and admit to being used analogously on the horizontal level. Let us look more closely however at *graduated* significance.

The Qualification of the Model. The positive and analogous model, taken from ordinary, non-religious language, needs to be 'qualified'.7 This occurs in ever-expanding stages, until the point where the significance of the word in question has been expanded to infinity.

The term in question must be usable in a comparative mode: *"more* merciful", and also "the father of *more* children".

The term in question must be usable in a progressive mode: *"More* merciful...*still more* merciful...*yet more* merciful"*;* also: "the father of *more and more* children".

The term in question must be usable in a *negative* way: *"not* so merciful *as* other merciful ones"; also: "not a father like other fathers".

The term in question must be used in *asinotic* mode:8 *"infinitely* more merciful", and also "the father of *all* in *every possible* respect". This is to say that the difference between "infinitely more merciful" and the immediately preceding "more merciful" cannot be expressed in any determinate fashion – that is: finitely – because the distance is itself *infinite.*

The term in question must be usable in a *transcendent* mode: *"infinitely merciful"*, and also "eternal Father". This is to say that "infinitely merciful" is *not* the summum of a series of 'merciful's', but is infinitely *beyond* the whole series.9

The Infinitizing of the Model. The "infinitization" of the meaning of a term is found not only in religious language, but is also fully acknowledged in other fields as well. In mathematics, for example, the *'limit'* is not only a wholly accepted term but is indispensable in certain branches. Moreover, the rules for its use are elaborate and recognized: the *3* is the limit of *2.9999....* The circle is the limit of the square.

In mathematics the movement towards a limit is quite elaborated. But this *infinitization* of meaning is not lacking in other types of discourse as well; even in poetry one finds it fairly frequently. And in the extrapolation of certain terms in the exact sciences one can discern something similar — a graduating movement towards an unspecifiable limit.

To be sure, this infinitization takes away the possibility of indicating with any precision both the passage from the progressive gradations to the actual limit itself, and the limit's distance from every preceding moment, since this distance is itself infinite. Nonetheless the direction of the infinitized meaning remains determinate: the circle is the limit of the square, not of the rectangle (whose limit would be an ellipse); in the same way, the 'infinitely merciful' and the 'infinitely good' do not coincide as concepts. They coincide in the divine *subject*.10

The "Revealed" Attributes

Regarding 'revealed attributes', and especially those concerning the Trinity, one needs logically to make a *second* infinitization– almost the reverse of the first – as a *restriction*.

'Father'. "Father of all", as well as "Father of his Chosen People", and even more: "Father of the King (David) and of the King's House", "Father of the Just"; and in a very special sense: "Father of Jesus" (John 20, 17), "Only Father of the Only Son".

'Son'. What occurs here is a process correlative to 'Father':
"All are sons (and daughters) of one divine Father" . . . "the only
son of the only Father".

'Spirit'. A two-step procedure is to be made here: both
from the scriptural meaning of 'Spirit' ("ruah", "pneuma" – *not* the
customary meaning of 'spirit' in our own languages), and from its
customary meaning *in* our languages: the *spirit* of a person, of a
people, of an era . . . performing first the 'infinitization' of the term,
and then the restriction to Christ and to the Father.

— And with regard to the special significance of other terms
which derive from 'Revelation': after performing the necessary
infinitization, one must explain their meaning in relation to the
'reductive' significance of Trinitarian terms.

The "Formal" Attributes

Certain terms used as predicates of the word "God" have,
at least in part, a significance which is formal-grammatical — they
function as a 'linguistic rule':

"God is good": in speaking of God, as we noted earlier, one
can only use 'positive' attributes and only negate 'negative' attributes.

"God is one": the word "God" is not used in the plural, except
in special contexts mentioned earlier.

"God is infinite": with regard to terms used as predicates of
"God" one must perform the 'infinitization'.

"God is transcendent": for terms used as predicates of "God"
one must go 'beyond' the infinite series of the infinitization.

THE SPECIAL CASE OF "GOD EXISTS"

If "being" is taken in its ancient and medieval sense as
"perfection", then it is an attribute, which is to say, a predicate: then
the process of infinitization can even be applied to the attribute "being
", right up to "esse subsistens", "actus (essendi) purus". If "being"
is taken in this sense – as an attribute subject to gradations – then
the ontological argument, beginning with the "the id quod maius
cogitari debet" and "id quo maius cogitari nequit," is possible but
fails to demonstrate actual existence.11

If on the other hand, "being" is taken as "actual existence", then it is *not* a predicate, as Kant saw clearly, and thus it is necessary to treat it in another context.12

CONCLUSION

What we say about God — the 'names of God' — are human names, words that belong to human discourse, but when they are used to refer to God, their significance is 'qualified' to the infinite. In this sense, the "logic of the attributes of God" *presupposes* the normal logic of human language: it does not render superfluous but indeed contains it; however it is distinct from it and surpasses it. The infinite 'extendability' of human meaning thus guarantees not only the religious significance but also, though secondarily, the specifically Christian significance.

The "logic of the attributes of God" directly determines the functioning of Christian communication, as we shall see in chapter Six.

And the infinite extension of human meaning has a correlative even in human existence itself, as we shall see in chapter Eight.

NOTES

1. This holds true also *indirectly* for the words deliberately coined for the purpose of speaking about God. The "possest", invented by Nicholas Cusanus as the exclusive attribute of God, presupposes the ordinary significance of the Latin *"posse"* ("to be able") and *"est"* ("he is") in order to say about God that "He is all that is able". Cfr. Nicolas Cusanus, *De possest*.

2. Ian Ramsey, *Religious Language : An Empirical Placing of Theological Phrases* (London, SCM Press, 1957). Especially: Chapter 2: "Some Traditional Characterizations of God: Models and Qualifiers," pp. 49ff.

3. Ramsey, however, does not speak of "the meaning of a word", but of a "situation": "A 'model' . . . is a situation with which we are all familiar, and which can be used for reaching another situation — with which we are not so familiar — one which, without the model, we should not recognize so easily". But he himself uses

as examples: "cause", "wise", "good", and "creation". Character Ramsey, *op cit*, p. 61ff.

4. Here and in what follows, "must" is obviously intended to be understood as a 'linguistic rule' ("Sprachregulung").

5. The term 'qualification' was introduced by Ramsey and is analogous to the logical term 'quantification': to any term "T" can be assigned either an *existential* quantification (T = "there exists at least one T") or a *universal* quantification (T = "for all T's"). But in the case of the use of a given term with respect to God, 'qualification' is that of the *infinitization* of the term's meaning. Cfr. Ramsey, *op cit*, p. 62.

6. Cfr. Karl Huber, "Zeichen Gottes - Zeichen der Kirche," Wilhelm Sandfuchs, *die Kirche* (Würzburg, Verlage Echter, 1978), pp. 11-24.

7. Cfr. Ramsey, *op.cit.,* p. 62.

8. The term 'asintotic' is borrowed from the geometry of the hyperbole, that is, of a curve whose shape approaches ever nearer to a right angle. Its 'asintotic' however is achieved only at *infinity.*

9. Cfr. Plato, *Symposium;* 209e-211c; Thomas Aquinas, *S.T.,* I. q. 2, a. 3.

10. And they coincide in him in a simple mode, with no composition or division, although for us this mode remains incomprehensible.

11. Cfr. Appendix.

12. See chapter 8: The justification for speaking about God 'realistically'.

CHAPTER SIX

THE ROLE OF THE "DIVINE NAMES" IN CHRISTIAN COMMUNICATION[1]

LEVELS OF LINGUISTIC MEANING IN CHRISTIAN COMMUNICATION

All forms of communication which are specifically Christian –catechesis, for example, but also theological study – occur on three distinct linguistic levels: the human, the religious, the Christian. The same word ("peace", "father", "love"), the same symbol (water, oils, bread) have *three* meanings, interrelated but distinct: a human or "lay" significance, a religious transcendent significance, and a specifically Christian significance.

For example, "father"

I. Common, "lay" level
transition:
a) acquisition of a positive significance
b) acquisition of a multivalent, *analogous* significance "father" in its everyday sense

II. Transcendent- religious level
transition:
a) *universalization:* father of more, and more, and more children --> of all children.
b) *totalization:* father in an ever-increasing number of respects --> in all respects.
  "father" of *all* in *every* respect

III. Christian level
translation:
limitation: Father more and more . . . specifically.
Only "Father" of the *Only* Son, eternal;
"Our "Father", as brothers and sisters of His *only* Son.

There is a twofold dynamic at work here: an *ascending* from the level of human significance to the Christian, and a *descending* from the level of Christian significance to the human.

As we see in the table, there is a twofold dynamic in Christian communication, especially in catechesis, which is operative at three linguistic levels. The fundamental dynamic is the first one, the descending dynamic. This is *theological* and descends from the Christian message to its human comprehension and realization. Given that the Christian message comes to *us* in words, and subsequently in symbols (sacraments and others), the descendent dynamic must continue to the point of *human experience.*[2] This theological dynamic is fundamental for catechesis, because faith does not come from human experience or reflection, but from listening to the Word of God.

The second dynamic ascends: from the customary significance of our words and, ultimately, our human experience, towards the hearing and acceptance of the Word of God; this dynamic is *pedagogical.*[3]

In preparing his instructions the catechist has to proceed by the first dynamic — the theological. One must begin with the Christian message, which must be considered in its 'global' aspect, and not only in its particularities. But at the same time one must reach the level of *human* significance, be it of the child, the student, or the adult.

In practical catechesis, on the other hand, the ascending, *pedagogical* dynamic comes to the fore. This is especially important when the catechesis is part of a *general* education process, where the catechesis, or better: an education in the Christian faith, is one of several activities or moments which themselves are not specifically religious. Even here one proceeds according to the *order* of the dynamic. As far as possible one must begin from the human significance recognized by one's listener, bring that significance to infinity, and finally *concretize* that with a text or episode from the Bible.

A thoroughgoing Christian initiation needs both of these dynamics: the upward movement towards God, and the downward movement towards the human being.[4]

Let us look at some examples of these three levels of linguistic significance.

THE LEVEL OF 'LAY' SIGNIFICANCE

Not only the words but also the symbols that are used in the context of Christian faith and thus in religious education, have a profane significance before having a religious and Christian significance. The reason is simple: a religious significance – for example, *grace,* divine aid — cannot be directly explained. "No one has seen God."[5]   Thus, religious meaning is introduced into human language only *indirectly,* which is to say, departing from profane meanings and analogously to them. Obviously this is not necessarily to say that we are using identical words: "grace" can be explained by "help", as "to pray" can be explained by "to ask". Words which are used predominantly or exclusively in a Christian religious context (grace, penance, sacrament, Mass, Church, etc.) have a special need to regain their analogous profane significance, departing from which they can then be explained. Otherwise they actually cannot be understood, as unfortunately happens often enough in our present cultural-historical context. Thus in the working out of any type of catechesis, this profane significance generally needs to be presented in an explicit and conscious manner. This 'passage' should ordinarily constitute the *first* stage of any catechesis.

At the level of profane meaning, the expressions used in a faith context have a polyvalent significance. "Love", "aid", "pardon" are not univocal terms, and do not signify one sole thing but have a multitude of interrelated uses. They are *analogous* terms. Even the word "father" doesn't refer only to the biological parent but to the multiple functions of the figure we call "father": "Father of the nation", "adopted father", "spiritual father". Usually this polyvalence must be pointed out and explicated so as to overcome the one-dimensionality of teenager speech; for them "love" often has only one association, and "help" can simply mean "give money".

Moreover, one must keep in mind that the expressions which in one way or another refer to God need to have a *positive* connotation. Thus if the word "father" has acquired a negative emotional freight in a particular case, one must make that conscious. Only then can a positive sense of the word be recognized and recovered. "God is a different kind of father.""What kind of father would you like to have?" Other examples of this problem are: "humility", "lord", "servant", etc.

THE LEVEL OF RELIGIOUS TRANSCENDENT MEANING

The meaning of a phrase to be used in speaking about God must be capable of being gradually stretched to infinity:

"Lord": "Lord of all the people —> for always —> Lord of all peoples —> Lord of all creatures —> in all possible respects";

"Father": "Father of the nation" —> father of all people —> "father of all creation —> in all possible respects";

"salvation": "God saves us not only from this or that danger, but from all and definitively";

"liberation": "God frees us not only from political or economic servitude, or from neurotic complexes, etc., but from sin, from every lack of liberty";

"bread": "bread of *eternal* life"; "bread for the life of the *world":* "eucharistic bread".

Without this expansion of the word's or symbol's meaning — an expansion to the infinite, the absolute and total — that which is told about Jesus remains at a human level: just one lovely story among so many others. Only if Christ is *God* must one choose life or death before Him.

A *direct* passage from the profane, human level to the Christian is not however possible. And thus the message of the Gospels cannot be truly comprehended without the mediation of the Old Testament — in whose gradual 'pedagogy' we see the passage from a profane (religious-reductive) level of meaning to one which is religious-absolute.[6] Catechesis thus demands a competent and ongoing use of the Old Testament. The concept of the Creator and the figure of Father must be presented in a clear manner alongside the figure of Christ and the concept of Lord.

THE LEVEL OF CHRISTIAN SIGNIFICANCE

To express the specific contents of the Christian message, the religious and transcendent significance of certain words and symbols must be applied or at least placed in relation to Christ. This application constitutes a final linguistic passage that changes the meaning of the words and symbols in question: Christ is God, and thus the significance of words used in relation to God are also true of Him.

But Christ is also a human being such as we, and thus the meaning of words used about one of us are also true of Him: to live, to love, to be near, to forgive. In the language employed in catechetical work one needs to continually present this *twofold value* of every word and symbol that refers to Christ, God and man.

God is the father of all human beings and therefore also the Father of Jesus. We all are sons and daughters of God and so also Jesus is Son of God. Already in the Old Testament we begin to find *gradations* in the significance of certain words. The king, the holy one, the "servant of Yahweh", etc., are children of God in a *special* way, and God is Father in a *special* way of the Jews, of the House of David, of the King, of the holy one, of the prophet, of the "servant of Yahweh". Moreover, Jesus is "Son of God" in a manner different from all the rest of us, in a way that is special, unique.[7] Precisely here arises the *new* way with which we too, brothers and sisters of Jesus, are children of the Father, and among ourselves we are all, in a way which is *new,* brothers and sisters.

If this passage from the religious and transcendent level to the *specifically Christian* dimension of God is not made, then speaking about Christ, and consequently of everything he did, and of all that refers to him in the Gospels, and of the profound, absolute and transcendent significance of Christian faith and life, remains incomprehensible.

On the contrary, only by seeing the Absolute and Infinite in Jesus can I then discover the same in the Church, in the events of history, in my own life, and in my brothers and sisters.

NOTES

1. The preceding chapter has not exhausted the logic of the attributes of God. We will develop this theme now, even at the cost of some repetition, in the present chapter, examining the matter from a diferent angle — that of communication.

2. We will take up this aspect in the next chapter.

3. In calling this dynamic 'pedagogical', we are reaching back to a very ancient precedent: The Alexandrine Fathers, especially Clement, called both the Old Testament and Greek

philosophy "paidagogos" — a pedagogy on the part of God which was to lead to Christ.

4. At various points in the development of a mature and personal faith, one or the other dynamic will be dominant. In catechetical work at the parish level the theological, descendent aspect will predominate, and this is all the more true at the level of academic instruction. But in work with youth groups or within the family it is generally the pedagogical, ascending dynamic which prevails.

The essential complementarity of the two movements is the reason why a truly thoroughgoing faith education has need of diversified and distinct 'agents': school, parish, youth group, family. In some cases, one of these agents must make up for the lack of another; but in no case should any one of them have a monopoly. Equally unfortunate is the attempt to create an alibi for oneself: "The school will take care of it; the parish will take care of it."

5. John 1: 18.

6. We shall return to this consideration in Chapter 7.

7. John 20, 17.

RELIGIOUS LANGUAGE

PART III

THE PRAGMATICS OF FAITH

CHAPTER SEVEN

EXPERIENCE, SYMBOL AND CONCEPT — THEIR SPECIFIC FUNCTION IN RELIGIOUS LANGUAGE

EXPERIENCE — SYMBOL — CONCEPT [1]

Both the language and the meaning of all that we say is connected to human experience, individual or collective. This is true also, and in a special way, of religious language.

Many aspects of the problem of the actual dependence of linguistic meaning on human experience can be left to psychology and philosophical anthropology. There is however a concrete dependence of conceptual knowledge on experience that is especially important for us: that which is necessarily mediated by symbols.

Experience

As instances of human experience which are of interest to us here let us take the following examples which are simple, very common, yet fundamental:

to be hungry and to eat food, for example, bread;
to be thirsty and to drink water;
to experience darkness and to see light;
to be cold and to feel the warmth of a fire;
to be dirty and to bathe.

These are 'total' experiences, in the sense that they involve the human psychophysical unity as such. Hunger, thirst, darkness, warmth, are corporally experienced through our senses. But since hunger, thirst, cold, are *experiences,* the human being is conscious of them, even if in diversified ways.

These are specifically *human* experiences, not only because they are generally conscious, but also by virtue of their content. To be sure, they are found in many animals — not in all! — but in the human being they form part of a behavior which is not only natural but also *cultural.* The preparation of food and drink, the cultural diversity in farming methods, cooking, dwelling and clothing, even in the use of fire. In other words, even the most simple and fundamental experiences that we human beings have, we have *learned* to have within an 'ensemble' of human behaviors, that are only *in part* determined by natural biological and psychological factors. Indeed, insofar as they are *human* experiences they depend all the more on cultural factors. Thus these experiences are integrated in a structure of *meanings,* which constitute, so to speak, a 'text'.

The experiences of thirst, hunger, light, etc., can be particularly strong: after a long journey without water, thirst can be acute, and the first glass of water is delicious. After a day of fasting, hunger can be acute, and in eating a morsel of bread one discovers the special flavor of bread; after a demanding walk one is particularly tired and dirty, such that upn showering or better: taking a dip in the sea, one knows the freshness and softness of water, and dressing in clean clothes one feels renewed.

Notwithstanding, however, that human experiences are determined by cultural factors, they cannot be *communicated,* especially when one is dealing with strong and profound experiences. One can only *recount* a personal experience. An experience is had in the first person, even if it can be made in a group. The personal experience in itself is not communicable.[2]

When I listen to another's account of his experience, I can myself experience something which is for me strong and profound, but it will always be a *different* experience from the one recounted to me.[3]

On the other hand what can be done (and in religious and also moral education *should* be done, especially with young children and youth) is to create the conditions and situations in which others can have their *own* experience.

The Symbol

A deep experience of hunger, thirst, darkness can acquire a profundity that surpasses the ordinary aspect of this experience, especially if my powers are reduced to the point where I am afraid, where I understand that if I do not eat and drink something I will die. Then my whole existence depends on water, bread, fire. I can also be so utterly filthy and stink so badly that I become repulsive to myself, and I regain my human dignity only by bathing and donning fresh clothing. In such situations it is not a matter of *this* hunger, this thirst, this filth; of *this* bread, this water, this fire, but of something *total,* absolute: this hunger, thirst, etc., comes to represent *all* hunger, even all desire. This bread, this water source, this fire *represent* life, happiness, and so on. My hunger and thirst is for *life,* I want to be *free,* I seek to recover *youth.*

In this way my powerful experiences acquire a *symbolic* value. Thirst, hunger, no longer refer only to this thirst, this hunger. They refer to something larger, more profound and total: the experiences have a *meaning* that transcends them, even if this meaning is *not yet* apprehended precisely and reflectively.

If, moreover, this powerful experience is accompanied by words or by a gesture which is explicit and conscious, an authentic and specific symbol is born. Coming at last upon a spring, for example, I can refrain from drinking first so as to offer the opportunity to another. Or the last piece of bread is shared by all in the group. In such cases the source of water, the piece of bread, the fire, are *used* in a conscious way to express something more, something other than itself. "This water is an expression of my friendship", "this bread we share is a sign of our community".

The difference between the meaning-value of the kind of powerful experience of which we have been speaking, and that of an authentic and specific symbol does not depend on the greater awareness and precision of the latter, but lies in the fact that the symbol is accompanied by a gesture, and by means of this gesture is part of what can be called a *rite.*[4]

This placement within a rite confers a *repeatability* on the symbol, guaranteeing it a preliminary *communicability,* or better: the possibility of being *shared.* By its nature a symbol is communitarian and intersubjective. It lives not in the mind of an individual, as an experience does, but in a constituted group, even if only a small one. Indeed, there are family symbols, even symbols between a pair of lovers, or friends.

But for a symbol to be *intersubjective* it must be intersubjective from the beginning. As our examples show, the birth of a symbol, however powerful the experience behind it, always requires the intervention of *another*, even if only one other individual. But he/she doesn't intervene as simply another individual, as simply 'subjectivity', with his or her 'personal experience', but as a member of a group within which a rite is constituted — we might say: within which the rules of a 'game' are determined.

For this reason, "I" do not count by virtue of my experience in my subjectivity, but by virtue of my being the 'other' to another. Nor does this deprive the other of his subjectivity — his being a subject, an "I"; indeed his being an "I" for me, and my being an "I" for him, are the conditions of possibility for *any* intersubjective communication. Without a common and commonly lived world of language and symbols[5] another cannot be another "I" for me, and I cannot be one for him. In different terms: only when together we begin to play according to the rules are we constituted as *subjects* and able to communicate *intersubjectively*. Edmund Husserl elaborated this in his famous Fifth Cartesian Meditation.[6] The constitution of a world for consciousness is the condition of possibility for the constitution of another "I" for this consciousness. It follows then that an *immediate* relation between subjects is not possible and that the mediation between *subjects as such* cannot be itself subjective but is, above all symbolically objective.

The Concept

Without the words which express it an experience, however profound, cannot be confronted. Only the words that conceptualize and generalize the experience render it really *communicable* and permit an *encounter.*[7] Without a concept, therefore, my experience cannot even have a meaning for me; it vanishes and I immediately forget it. Thus I have no possibility of *verifying* it. Without a concept I can have no fear of darkness, for example; nor can I be hungry for something — indeed, there isn't even any *hunger,* but only a kind of suffering.

A symbol then without a concept is not understood, and loses its symbolic power. This is to say that symbols have need of *explication.* Only the *words* that impart a determinate significance to them integrate them in a clear context of communication.
In this way a symbol born of experience acquires a *universal* value and can be *repeated*. We divide bread among ourselves even when

we are *not* hungry, and we do it every time we come together.

APPLICATION TO THE MEANING OF CHRISTIAN RELIGIOUS LANGUAGE

"An experience without a concept is blind; a concept without an experience is empty."[8] This is especially true in the domain of religion, and particularly so for the Christian faith, insofar as it is a *revealed* faith. But given that we can never have a *direct* experience of God in this life, nor of all that is expressed in the literal meaning of religious language, only the kind of profound experience described above can in some way give a content to the concepts of Christian language. Precisely because the *specific content* of religious and Christian language cannot be experienced directly, the recognition and the meaningfulness of the *symbol* for religious language in general and Christian language in particular becomes utterly essential.

We should recall however that already at the ordinary level of the consciousness and meaningfulness of language, the necessary order is: *experience* à *symbol* à *concept*, and not: *experience* à *concept* (idea) à (which is then expressed by means of a) *symbol.* The symbol is not the expression of an idea or a concept by means of an abstraction from the concreteness of an experience, but is the *mediation* from the experience to the concept.

At this point a diagram similar to the one given earlier for the three levels of meaning, will be helpful:

HUNGER   *BREAD*   *EATING*

1. MOMENT OF THE EXPERIENCE

passage:
a deepening within consciousness of ordinary experience:

strong hunger   *last piece of bread*   *the taste of bread*

2. SYMBOLIC MOMENT

passage:

the significance of an experience which has been undergone is
expressed:

strong hunger   last piece of bread   sharing it with another

3. CONCEPTUAL MOMENT

passage:
the meaning of the symbol and of the experience becomes
determinate.

(This thus includes an initial reflection upon the experience by way
of ascertaining it)

strong hunger[9]   *piece of bread   sharing it with another,
saying: "This is a sign of our love."*

        In the case of Christian language the *mediation* between
experience and concept-word is *not* a mediation from experience
to concept, but rather a 're-mediation' *from* the concept-word *to*
the experience! The specific meanings of the Christian faith are
given to us by way of a *message,* a revelation, a *Word* — that of
the Sacred Scriptures and tradition.[10]
        Precisely for this reason the function of the symbol for the
comprehension of the specific significance of Christian language
becomes even more important and indispensable; one can think here
of the sacraments, the various rites and the whole liturgy. What
occurs *by means of* these symbols is that the message of the faith
is linked to and placed within human experience. One needs though
to keep in mind the *double* mediating function of the symbol: that
which begins with the *Word,* and that which begins from *experience.*

CONCLUSION

        The function of the symbol for human intelligence is
essential. The symbolizing capacity of the human intellect *frees*
thought from its reputed[11] total dependence on experience and
confers upon thought its *creativity,* whether in art or in mathematics.
Only through the mediation of the symbol is human thought open to

the infinite and to transcendence – which is to say, one can think even that which is not experiential. It is precisely through the mediation of the symbol that thought is *really* open to the infinite and to transcendence.[12] It follows then that one can think *God* and speak about Him. But it also follows that thinking *God* and speaking about Him necessitates the mediation of the symbol.

NOTES

1. Cfr. Carlo Huber, *Critica del Sapere*, 20.5, pp. 331-336.

2. Cfr.. Huber, *Critica del Sapere*, pp. 114-118 and 137-141.

3. This last observation is critically important in the acceptance of religious and moral truths — for example: in the comprehension and reception of an episode form the Gospels. To listen to the Gospel proclamation, especially when it is proclaimed as the "Word of God", can in certain circumstances constitute a strong and profound religious experience, but *not* necessarily. In *no* case however will the listener's experience be that of the Apostles when, for instance, they encountered the risen Lord. As its foundation faith has not our experience, but rather a *testimony*, a witness, that becomes accepted as true. On the other hand, every acceptance of a religious faith, and even every *authentic* acceptance of an ethical value, needs to be *personally experienced* — this is called a 'religious experience', a 'faith experience', a 'moral experience', but it remains forever a *personal experience*, incommunicable as such, similar to a profound *sense* experience.

4. Note that here we are not so much concerned with significance or with specifically *religious* symbols. Powerfulness, profundity and breadth of meaning are found also at the profane and 'lay' level; indeed, in a certain sense they are found here in the first place.

5. This not only does not cast doubt upon the reality of the world, but presupposes it.

6. Husserl, *Cartesianische Meditationen und Pariser Vorträge*, vol. 1 (Haag: Husserliana, 1963).

7. The communicability of the symbol is merely an *preliminary* communicability.

8. Kant, *Critique of Pure Reason*, A 51.

9. In this conceptual moment the originary experience can be quite distant. Where the symbol is *a* symbolical *action* ("*dividing the last piece of bread*", etc.) the conceptual clarification is often given by the situation and has no need of words.

10. *Conc.Trid.* sesssion IV (Denz. 1501) : "hanc veritatem et disciplinam contineri in libris scriptis et sine scripto traditionibus".

11. In this consists the radical error of every empiricist theory of consciousness, especially the conception of language put forth by Locke. Cfr. *Essay Concerning Human Understanding*, Book III, "Of Words".

12. Perhaps the limit of Kant's thought consists precisely in this, that he has not seen the symbolizing function of the sensible 'schematism'. Cfr. Kant, *Critique of Pure Reason*, B 177ff.

CHAPTER EIGHT

THE JUSTIFICATION FOR SPEAKING ABOUT GOD REALISTICALLY

Introduction

If the symbolical mediation from experience to thought gives to the latter its creative liberty, it also places it at the junction between truth and falsehood: one can think that which does not exist, and even more: one can think that which *cannot* exist. Lewis Carroll's Red Queen, every morning before breakfast, thought seven impossible thoughts.[1] We can err and we can lie.[2]

Obviously this is also and in a special way true for that which we say about God. The sheer diversity of religions is the visible confirmation of this. The fact that one can speak about God does not guarantee the existence of God. The ontological argument for the existence of God, whether Anselm's[3] or Descartes'[4] or even less Bonald's[5], is not valid. The mere existence of Christian discourse about God is no guarantee of the truth of the Christian faith. On the other hand, not only Christians but other religions as well lay claim to the truth of that which they say about God. This is particularly true in the case of the foundational assertion of every religion: that God exists. It cannot be the task of a logical or phenomenological analysis to *demonstrate* the existence of God. Another philosophical method would be needed for that. On the other hand, it is the proper task of logical and phenomenological analyses to determine what *sense* and what *importance* a "demonstration of the existence of God" has, and what its *role* is within Christian discourse about God.

THE REALISTIC SENSE OF CHRISTIAN DISCOURSE ABOUT GOD

When a believing Christian says something about God, he intends what he says in a real way: not only the historical facts essential to the 'Salvation story" (the life, the death, and the resurrection of Jesus), but also that which he says *about* God is

intended *realistically*, especially the assertion of God's existence.[6]
Every *non-realistic* "interpretation" – psychological, mythological,
philosophical, etc. – changes totally the meaning of the whole
discourse to the point where the specifically *religious*
meaningfulness of the discourse is lost.[7]

On the other hand, the realism of Christian discourse is not an
empirical realism: in the expression "God exists", the word *exists*
does not have the same sense it has in "Kangaroos exist" (in
Australia) or "Dinosaurs existed" (millions of years ago) or
"Subatomic particles exist"; nor does it have the same sense as
"Unicorns exist" (in fable) or "Frodo exists" (in literature). The
word *exist* is an *analogous* term.[8] To speak of God in a Christian
sense, which is to say, realistically, means to accept a meta-empirical
reality, non-sensible, non-experiential[9] yet nonetheless real and
factual.[10] At the same time, the realistic meaning of Christian
discourse about God, especially the assertion of the real existence
of God, *demands a link*, a connection of some kind to experience.
Such a link to experience is necessary for all human thought which
would otherwise be lost in fantasy.

THE ANALOGICAL LINK TO THE TOTALITY OF HUMAN EXPERIENCE (IN REALISTIC DISCOURSE ABOUT GOD)

For the analogical connection between *realistic* discourse about
God, on the one hand, and the *totality* of human experience, on the
other, we must turn to that which we said earlier concerning *models*.
This time, however, we will use the term 'model' not for the linguistic
significance of a known word, but for special situations[11] wherein
a *horizon* is *opened up*.

The Opening of a Horizon

There is a phenomenon specific to human intellectual life which
goes by a variety of names used analogously: "the opening of the
horizon", which borrows the term *horizon* from Husserl; "alteration
in the state of consciousness", inspired by Kant and by psychology;

"intellectual conversion", which uses a term of Christian faith but makes it available for an analogous use. These expressions all describe a rather common phenomenon in life and in human intellectual development. I.T. Ramsey calls it 'disclosure' or sometimes 'discernment'. [12]

Let us say that one meets a person for the first time of whom one has already heard much and about whom one already possesses a good deal of information. In the meeting, one may not acquire 'new' information, yet *all* that is already known takes on a new meaning.

After having listened to many musical fragments, one hears a particular selection and says: "Now I understand Bach" or "classical music" or "jazz".

One finally manages to solve a particular type of mathematical problem and one says, "Now I've got it." And in fact from now on he or she is able to solve other problems of this type. In these and similar examples it is not so much the matter of a single experience but rather that *in* this particular experience one comprehends a whole, a totality: a new *horizon* is opened. [13]

These openings of new horizons have a certain similarity with the 'powerful experiences' discussed in the preceding chapter, in which a symbolical repeatability is born.   Here too, this phenomenon of the opening of a new horizon or an alteration in the state of consciousness needs to be *conceptualized and 'tested'*. A part of this 'testing' or verification consists in the possibility of acquiring and subsequently understanding the rules of the language game under consideration — in this case, the interrelated rules of Christian discourse about God.

All-Inclusive and Infinitely Open Horizons

Obviously the examples we have just used pertain to finite and limited horizons. The horizon within which one can realistically speak about God, within which even an *act of faith* in God is possible, must necessarily be a horizon which is open and unlimited. There are horizons which by their nature are unlimited: one's own life[14] , one's consciousness[15] , knowledge, history, the universe, and also intersubjectivity and language, especially freedom. It would be almost better to say: these horizons *can and must* be unlimited, since they are all too often thought of as finite and limited, and one needs to show the contradictory nature and even the absurdity of the latter notion.[16] Not only is this possible but it constitutes an essential passage for the opening-up of a horizon within which one can speak realistically about God.

The Opening of an Unlimited Horizon and the Semantic Universe. The issues involved in the opening of an unlimited horizon can be seen very well within the context of the ontological argument of St. Anselm.

The true atheist does not deny God, but in fact doesn't think Him. He moves in a *different* semantic universe, a universe where there is no place for the terms "id quo maius cogitari nequit" and "id quod maius cogitari debet". How is one to demonstrate the inevitability of a true concept of God? One needs to *open up a horizon* within which the word "God" has a possible use, even a necessary use — and then to demonstrate that this horizon is a necessary condition for the possibility of any speech and all thinking.[17] This is precisely what Kant did with regard to "the ideal of pure reason" – that is, the idea of God – demonstrating that the regulative use of "the ideal of pure reason" is a necessary condition for the possibility of any reasoning process.[18]

Since a semantic universe is at the same time a socio-cultural reality, the task of changing, enlarging or opening up such a universe is surely an educational and catechetical task. Even so, the opening of a new dimension of thinking is still a primarily philosophical task.[19] Now if what Wittgenstein says is true, that "the limits of language are the limits of my world"[20], then a change from one semantic universe in which the expression "God" or rather, "id quo maius cogitari nequit", has neither use nor sense, to another semantic universe where this expression possesses both a meaning and a use, implicates a change of the whole world and the whole life.

How is such a change possible? Wittgenstein says: "The world of the happy is another world than that of the unhappy."[21] And again: "If a good or bad will can change the world, what it changes is only the limits of the world."[22]

Now, is the change from a linguistic universe that does not include the expression "id quo maius cogitari nequit" to one which includes it a moral act, an act of freedom, that constitutes the whole of a world? Or will it be — *also* — a salvific act of God that redeems and restores language from its fallen state and from its continued tendency to fallenness, as He has redeemed human social nature and freedom?[23]

The 'Center' or 'Limit' of a Limitless Horizon

The *opening up* of an unlimited horizon is not itself sufficient for the passage from a universe where the word "God" has no sense to one where this word possesses a realistic significance. In Christian discourse about God, as well as in the discourse of other religions, the word 'God' does not refer to any horizon however unlimited, but directs one *beyond* it. God is neither freedom, nor the order of the world, nor the rationality of history; nor is He (except in a very analogous way which must be carefully qualified) the meaning of life. We already examined this in Chapter Five with regard to the attributes of God: their *significance* is not the *summum* or the culmination of an infinite series; their significance is rather the transcendent God who is beyond any infinite series. The word 'God' is used to refer to One who is totally *distinct* from every other thing, even from every totality, be it ever so unlimited.

All this notwithstanding we do speak about God, and the word "God" is *part of human language*. Moreover, we speak about God using ordinary linguistic tools — religious language is *not* a special language which is to be distinguished from the everyday language we use otherwise. God, as that who is beyond language and beyond every unlimited horizon as well, nevertheless *belongs to* and is found *within* this one. Otherwise we would not be able to speak about God and He would remain completely inconceivable. In that case Wittgenstein would be right in saying: "*As* the world is, it is a matter of absolute indifference to whatever is higher than it.

God is not made manifest *in the world.*"[24] Indeed in the language of the *Tractatus'* logical atomism one cannot speak of God.[25] In the Christian faith, however, and in other monotheistic religions, God is conceived not only as beyond all, but also as distinct from every single reality of this world. This is precisely what has already been seen in the similarity of the word "God" to other proper names and in the membership of this term "God" within the group of terms having a unique reference[26] . The word "God" is, so to speak, a 'pro-nome' which points and refers beyond itself.

For this reason the place of God within the manifold of possible unlimited horizons cannot be simply *any* place – on the same plane with and similar to the place of other realities. God's place within the horizon can only be the *center*, which is a special position, unlike any other position.

The center of a circle is in fact *not* a point in the circle, but is the origin of the circle, or its total concentration; within the Cartesian system its coordinates are $x=0; y=0$.

Geometric and Pictorial Figures

In other words, that which is beyond the series, beyond any and every series, reveals itself as the center. This is what we saw in Chapter Four: the word "God" is not simply one word among the other words used in religious discourse but is this discourse's semantic center, determining the specific sense in which all religious language is used. To better understand how it is that the 'center' of an unlimited horizon can and indeed must be conceived as beyond this very horizon – or: how it is that that which is beyond a horizon can manifest itself as its center – we can examine two analogous situations, one geometric, one pictorial. Nicholas Cusanus argued the 'conjunction of opposites' in God, illustrating the correspondence between 'infinitum maximum' and 'infinitum minimum', and brought in the geometric analogy of the circle, better still: the 'infinite sphere'[27] and its center: in this case the circumference is not located at any particular position and the center is everywhere.[28]

More or less at the same time as Cusanus lived, the artists of the Renaissance, rediscovered perspective, making use of it in sophisticated and symbolical forms.[29] The perspective in a painting goes beyond the painting towards infinity, but departs from its perspective center –the figure in which coincide not only the attention of the viewer but also, in Christian iconography, the sense of the infinite: for example, the face of Christ in DaVinci's Last Supper, or the host in Raphael's Dispute over the Eucharist. The center, which as limit both belongs and does not belong to the complex of forms and figures, brings all the figures and forms into focus.

Beyond the Horizon

After this rather theoretical exposition, we must turn to the existential and experiential level. If a Christian, or any monotheist, wants to give to the word "God" a realistic meaning the unlimited horizon *needs* a center, and that which is beyond the horizon must manifest itself as its center. Thus one can say: my entire life has a sense; the story has an end; the universe has a cause; freedom is a call, and so on.

This is the reason why the pure fact of limitless and open horizons is not sufficient. This fact does indeed guarantee the possibility of speaking, thinking, being free, etc. But at this level of consciousness this opening remains merely *implicit*. For it to become explicit demands the *awareness* of a center. Reciprocally, in order to individualize a *center* in an limitless horizon at least a preliminary awareness is necessary — an awareness of the openness and the limitlessness of the respective horizon, the *discovery* of the horizon *as* open and limitless.[30]   Otherwise I remain unaware of it and I am unable to say: "My life has a sense."

But it is important to notice that these limitless horizons are *not* discovered to be self-grounding; rather they are discovered as simply *given*. If this then gives them a reality for consciousness it does not give them a grounding or foundation, certainly not in consciousness itself.

Only a center to their very limitlessness, which at the same time is beyond it, gives them their limitlessness, gives them a ground or foundation,[31] which as a result guarantees also their oppenness. Without such a transcendental center these horizons close up.[32]

The mere discovery, however, of the limitlessness of these horizons is not a simply intellectual act, and even less does it give any indication of their center. These depend at least in part on the *will,* and belong within the domain of *choices.*[33] Nonetheless we are dealing here with reasonable and often well-reasoned choices. Thus it is quite possible for the discovery process to occur during a course of *study,* especially the study of philosophy, even if afterwards one speaks more of an 'intellectual conversion'. In any event, the process has both elements of *experience* and elements of *reasoning*. Here again Kant's dictum is quite applicable: "The concept without experience is empty; the experience without the concept is blind."[34]

The traditional "proofs for the existence of "God"" form
the logical skeleton of an intellectual process. But without the
experience of a real opening up of a limitless horizon and then the
further identification of its center, the arguments are mere bones
without flesh. Precisely for this reason these proofs can be logically,
speculatively and philosophically *valid*, but *alone* they generally
remain *unconvincing*.

The Identification with "God"

One essential move is still missing for a full rational
justification for speaking about God in a realistic way. Aquinas
does not conclude his *quinque viae* with: "Ergo Deus existet" but
with: "et hoc omnes *dicunt* Deum"![35] This last move is no longer
a forensic move, but a move in *semantic identification*.

Today this move is certainly more problematic than at the
time of Aquinas. Many today would not be inclined to consider "God"
as the "meaning of life". Precisely for this reason we need more
profound *information* as to the true significance of the word "God"
in Christian language.

We need to look again at the role and central function of
the word "God" in religious language.[36] Directly or indirectly, the
term "God" determines the entire semantic universe of religious
language, especially Christian language. The opening of a limitless
horizon and then the recognition of its center is, as we've discussed,
a process of discovery, a process of awareness, but the semantic
universe of religious language is a linguistic, semantic, social-cultural
and historical structure which *precedes* the process of awareness.
In a process of socialization and tradition, one comes to know and
learn both the semantic universe of religious language and the
structure of this universe as it is focused upon and determined by
the word "God".

If this identification is made in the first person[37] — "and
this I call 'God'" — it is certainly what J.H. Newman called a 'real
assent'.[38] The certainty of this identificative assent resides not in
the premises of an argumentation that can lead one merely to a
'notional assent', but in the 'real apprehension' of a limitless
horizon,[39] which for Newman is the horizon of moral obligation

that manifests itself in the conscience.[40]

If this identification is made by a believing Christian or by one who is progressing along a path towards faith, then this is something very near to an *act of faith*.[41]   If afterwards this identification proceeds to "God as Father of Christ", with the resulting partial substitutibility of the word "God" with the proper name "Jesus" as the fulcrum of the meaningfulness of religious language,[42] then one is explicitly dealing with the Christian faith.

THE LEVEL OF CONSCIOUSNESS FOR AN OPENING OF AN UNLIMITED HORIZON AND FOR THE IDENTIFICATION OF ITS CENTER AS "GOD"

This is an important problem not only philosophically but theologically, and also pedagogically.   Without the opening of an unlimited horizon and the identification of God the Father of Christ as its center, an act of faith is not possible. Without the conscious opening of an unlimited horizon it is not even possible to conceive of God. One could conceive of an idol, but not of God. We need then to ask ourselves what is the intellectual, emotional and moral level of maturity which furnishes the necessary condition for an authentic act of faith. Clearly we are not asking here about the *theological* conditions necessary for an act of faith; these are traditionally dealt with in an analysis of faith in the context of theology. Here we are asking about the human psychological conditions necessary for this faith act. And obviously the experience and thus the conscious opening of an unlimited horizon is different for an adult than for a child. We need therefore to begin with the fact that faith is *also* a reality which is *communitarian and social,* not only from a psychological point of view but from a theological: the faith in God and in Christ is always also faith in the Church, not only as regards what is believed but as regards the act through which one believes. Thus even the path towards faith, education in the faith, and finally the reasonability of the proclamation of the existence of God are always *also socializing processes.*

The Small Child

When one baptizes a child, the child is baptized in the faith of a church, and generally the church of the parents and godparents. For this reason the parents are justifiably required to participate in a special catechesis program prior to the baptism of their child. Within the family and in an atmosphere of faith the child in due course learns to use *also* the word "God" within the language which he or she learns in a process of linguistic socialization.

Elements of linguistic socialization and social behavior in general are present and necessary in any conversion. To believe in God is *never* a strictly personal act, anymore than knowing is. The problem, however, is the level of intellectual development a child must have for the opening up of a limitless horizon of a human life, the world, etc., and the subsequent apprehension of that horizon's center. An infant obviously has no such capacity and is thus incapable of an act of personal faith. But a child of six or seven?

Even a young child lives its life in a conscious way, and lives it in a world. The world of the little child is certainly *little*, but it is nonetheless a world which is whole and *total*. Moreover, the child quite consciously experiences its world as *continuously and concentrically increasing*. This is to say that the child grows, wants to grow, and grows consciously. This suggests that even the horizon of the life and the world of a child is *unlimited*. But the child does not experience this limitlessness in specific moments of the opening up of a horizon, except in rare cases.[43] However the child does experience this limitlessness not only through contacts with adults but for itself: in its curiosity that is continuous and insatiable, in its desire to grow. We are dealing here with an experience of limits and with an ongoing passing beyond these limits. This little but limitless horizon of the child has its own precise centerpoint: the center of the world of the child is *the child itself.* Young children are extreme ego-centrists — the word is not intended here in a moral sense. In order to center the horizon of its life in God the child needs guidance and stimulation on the part of adults, not only however on the level of linguistic-socialization (speaking to the child about God and Christ, teaching the child to pray, and so on). The child is also capable of a personal experience, and indeed has need of it. The experiences through which a child can discover the centrality of God in its own life are those which are linked to the child's life precisely in the child's own 'centrality', in its own ego-centrism. Such experiences can include those of wonder, of gratuitousness, of thankfulness.

In all of this the great imagination of the child does not constitute a danger but a help. The child sees things that are not seen, is forever playing, but knows well the difference between play and reality, between fable and truth. The child is a *realistic animal.*[44]

The School-Age Child

The intellectual situation of the school child is quite different from that of the pre-schooler. The school child does *not* live in a unified and complete world, and he himself, his personality and his life are not for him unified realities. His life and his world are multidirectional. In a certain sense he does not possess one unique horizon but a diversity of *partial* horizons that are not interrelated by an *interior* coherence: he lives in the family, goes to school, participates in sports, is part of a group, etc. He has many activities and an active schedule. In doing one thing, other things are forgotten.

Yet in some of these activities, in some of these directions — though not in all and not simultaneously — he continues to progress and make new discoveries, acquire new knowledge, and develop his capacities — if it pleases him. Each of his horizons is unlimited, but each is a partial horizon. He is in a certain sense a *technical animal.* Arguments to the effect that "a good grasp of mathematics will be necessary for your future life" make no sense to the school child. If he doesn't discover it himself, he will not bother himself about it unless through obedience or force. Yet in the activities which he pursues according to his tastes, he can remain extremely constant and obstinate to the death.

None of these partial horizons can be crystallized in God; even the faith of a school child has a technical aspect. Yet even in the area of faith the school child can develop a strong interest and make progress. Experiences of the opening up of horizons which are limitless and total are possible but very rare and when they do occur they tend to be fleeting.

The discourse of faith for a school child will be thus a discourse which is predominantly *socializing:* especially in the *belonging* to a group of peers. In a certain way these horizons substitute for a total horizon of one's life, of the world, etc. In this context the centrality of God can and must be realized in the *loyalty* to God as the loyalty to a group, to friends, etc. This can work however only if the identification with the group is, one the one hand strong, and on the other hand, personal — which is to say, if the identification is not just 'group-dependent'.

The Age of Transition

For the adolescent, the situation is difficult precisely because it is a situation of *transition*. Generally, the adolescent loses interest in a diversification of activities: "I don't want to play the piano anymore." *Particular* horizons cease to satisfy him. But the first step toward a possible and indeed necessary transition to horizons which are *total* — the future, life itself, and so on — is a crisis in the *particular* horizons. The adolescent no longer understands the world, nor others, nor himself. But exactly insofar as this crisis is itself total, it constitutes a limitless and universal horizon, even if in an empty and negative sense. The adolescent lives out a search for sense which he has so far not found, and he lives it out generally without the capacity to articulate it.[45]

The adolescent must be helped to discover this 'total crisis' as an opening to a universal and unlimited horizon, helped to articulate it; sometimes one must almost voice it for him. In such a context one finds the possibility to center the universal but still empty horizon in God, and to recover a discourse of faith.

Mature Faith

For a mature faith the opening of *one single* illimited horizon is not sufficient; various and interconnected horizons are necessary — all with their center in the *one* God, through whom then they find connection with one another: one's life, the future, communication, history, the world. What is wanted however are not all *possible* horizons, but the appropriate ones, whether for oneself or for others — at the appropriate moment.

THE LEVEL OF FAMILIARITY WITH CHRISTIAN RELIGIOUS LANGUAGE NECESSARY FOR THE IDENTIFICATION OF THE CENTER OF A UNLIMITED HORIZON WITH "GOD"

There is also a reverse side to this identification which needs to be addressed — namely, a competence in the semantic universe of religious language that has as the center of its meaningfulness the term "God". Here again we see important differences and variations, and we note its *graduality,* especially in the passage from an infantile faith to the faith of an adult.

With *no* knowledge of Christian religious language, of which "God" is the center, the term "God" itself has no Christian religious meaning. The knowledge can be minimal, but even a minimal competence must include factual elements: Biblical information, especially from the New Testament,[46] centered around the proper name "Jesus". Beyond this it must include moral elements, information about liturgical rites, prayer, etc. This knowledge is and remains a linguistic competence in a broad sense — *socialized,* acquired by means of a process of *learning.* The *progressive acquisition* of this knowledge needs to follow the parameters of general human intellectual development from infancy to adulthood, paying however special attention to the individual and to his personal and cultural circumstances.

CONCLUSION

In this last chapter we have not sought to give a demonstration of the existence of God, but a rational *justification* for a 'real assent', in Newman's sense, to the real existence of him whom Christians call "God", a justification which is also intellectually adequate to what St. Paul describes:

Faith gives substance to our hopes, and the conviction of realities we do not see.[47]

NOTES

1. Lewis Carroll, *Through the Looking Glass* (London:

Oxford, 1971).

2. For Umberto Eco the potential for use in lying is the definition of a sign. *A Theory of Semiotics* (Bloomington: Indiana University Press, 1976).

3. Anselm, *Prosologion,* chapters II and XV.

4. Descartes, *Meditationes de prima philosophia,* fifth meditation; ed. AT VII. pp. 65ff.

5. "Les hommes nomment Dieu, donc il est." De Bonald, M., *Legislation primitive,* 2 ed. (Paris, Le Clere, 1817); I. p. 379.

6. The assertion is indeed the *sine qua non* for whatever else is said about God.

7. See earlier, Chapter Four.

8. Thus even the term 'to exist' satisfies the condition of analogousness required for a term to be used as an *attribute* of God, even if 'to exist' cannot be gradated. However in the case of 'to exist' we are not dealing with an attribute in a *logical* sense.

9. In this sense it is not possible to be Christian *and at the same time* a thoroughgoing empiricist, materialist, positivist or even simply to negate the *possibility* of metaphysics.

10. Even the *existence* of the *idea* of God is not sufficient!

11. Ramsey originally used the term in this way. See Chapter Five, fn. XXX.

12. Cfr. Ramsey, *o.c.,* pp. 15ff.

13. For Ramsey this experience has something of the *instantaneous* about it: "The penny drops", "it dawns", etc. The similarity with the "ex aiphnes" of the *Symposium* 210e4 is most striking.

14. This is a witness to, though not a proof of, the belief concerning the immortality of the soul, of the person, of the consciousness, etc.

15. The ending or the 'death' of consciousness is not thinkable.

16. With regard to language and freedom, I have attempted to demonstrate this in: Huber, "Kirche: Zeichen Gottes — Zeichen der Freiheit"; in Wilhelm Sandfuchs, *Die Kirche* (Würzburg, Echter Verlag, 1978); pp. 11-24. With regard to language, see also: Carlo Huber, *Critica del Sapere;* pp. 203-223.

17. *Ibid.*

18. Cfr. Kant, *Critique of Pure Reason,* A 599-610.

19. One thus more easily understands why the Catholic Church requires the study of philosophy for those who wish to undertake theological studies for pastoral and missionary purposes.

20. *Tractatus*, 5.62.

21. *Tractatus*, 6.43.

22. *Tractatus*, 6.43.

23. Cfr. Huber, *op. cit.*, pp. 17 and 23f.

24. *Tractatus*, 6.432.

25. Cfr. *Tractatus*, 6.4: "All propositions are of equal value", and 6.41: "The sense of the world is outside of the world. In the world, all is as it is, and everything occurs as it occurs; there is in this no value. If there is a value that has value, then it must be outside of every occurence and every being-such. Every occurence and every being-such is accidental. Whatever would render them non-accidental cannot be in the world, which otherwise would in its turn be accidental. It must be outside of the world." However, as we saw in Chapter Two, Wittgenstein himself uses *another* language, an 'elucidating' language, in writing the *Tractatus*.

26. Cfr. Chapter Four above

27. Cfr. D. Mahnke, *Unendliche Sphäre und Allmittelpunkt* (Halle, 1937) (Facs. Nachdr. Fromann, Stuttgart-Bad Cannstatt 1966).

28. Cusanus, *op. cit.*, I, 4.11. According to I, 6.4, however, God is still beyond the conjunction of oppposites.

29. Cfr. Erwin Panowski, *Perspective as Symbolic Form* (New York: Zone Books; Cambridge, Mass.: distributed by the MIT Press, 1991).

30. We will consider below the intellectual and moral level necessary for at least a preliminary awareness of the various open and limitless horizons in a child, teenager, or adult.

31. Wittgenstein expresses this idea thus: "To contemplate the world sub specie eterni is to contemplate it as a — limited — whole. The intuition of the world as a limitless whole is the mystical." *Tractatus*, 6.45

32. Huber, Kirche, "Zeichen Gottes — Zeichen der Freiheit"; in Wilhelm Sandfuchs, *Die Kirche* (Würzburg, Echter Verlag, 1978), pp. 17, 23.

33. This would need to be elaborated in further detail in a phenomenology of the will, which however is not directly tied in

with our own reflections here on Christian discourse about God.

34. Kant, *Critique of Pure Reason*, A 51. Kant said literally: "Gedanken ohne Inhalt sind leer, Anschauungen ohne Begriffe sind blind."

35. Aquinas, *Summa Theologica,* I, q.2 a.3.

36. See Chapter Four.

37. If it is not made in the first person, it would sound: "and this is what Christians and others call 'God' (but not I, for I am an atheist)." In this case, the statement is purely semantic.

38. J.H. Newman, *An Essay in Aid of a Grammar of Assent,* I pt., Chapter 4.

39. Cfr. *Ibid.,* chapter III. "The apprehension of propositions" and their application to the field of religion in Chapter V: "Apprehension and Assent in the Matter of Religion, 1., Belief in One God."

40. *Ibid.,* "From the perceptive power which identifies the intimations of conscience with the reverberations or echoes (so to say) of an external admonition, we proceed on to the notion of a Supreme Ruler and Judge. . . ."

41. It is not yet the act of faith itself but its final presupposition, which however, in theological terms, is made only with the grace of God, and probably is made already in the light of faith itself. This is, so to speak, the ultimate logical presupposition that is comprehended in faith itself or that the faith pre-supposes for itself.

42. Cfr. Chapter Four.

43. There are instances of childhood mystical experiences. Cfr. Finn, *Hallo Mr. God, here is Anna.*

44. If Zubiri's definition of the human being as 'realistic animal' has any application at all, it is certainly to the child.

45. At a linguistic level we often encounter a rupture of linguistic codes among teenagers, an incommunicability, even a speechlessness and a kind of aphasia.

46. A knowledge of the contents of the Bible does not necessity require a *textual* knowledge.

47. Heb. 11:1.

CONCLUSION

We have made a long journey to the interior of the semantic universe of Christian religious language, both at the level of its contents and at the level of the methods which can be applied to it. We have seen that we are dealing with a universe which is complex but coherent. The structure of this universe guarantees it intelligible meaningfulness and also rationality. As centered in God, its very structure allows even a realistic acceptance of its meanings.

In an age such as ours, powerfully determined on the one hand by an emotional fideism, and on the other by a scientism which is equally emotional, a humble but persistent logical analysis of the faith is not only of critical importance for theology but also for the difficult task of evangelization and catechesis. For such an undertaking the tools of logical-linguistic analysis and phenomenology prove to be quite useful.

The philosophical importance of our analysis of Christian discourse about God consists in the fact that precisely the application of philosophy and its methods to discourse about God keeps us philosophers from making abortive or reductionist moves, and obliges philosophy finally to come to its own proper *limits* and to *think them*.

At the same time, discourse about God — and only this discourse — guarantees to language (and in consequence to philosophy) its *openness:* only if one can speak about "God", if there is a place for "God" in language, is the language open and alive; only if one poses the problem of God can philosophy avoid closing itself off in ideology.

Language is the medium par excellence of both information and communication. In both one says something *new*. Human progress and creativity also contain novelty. In language however the new can be expressed only if language is open-ended in all possible directions, that is, open infinitely. An openness for progress in *certain* directions and according to certain predetermined criteria is insufficient. Language can claim an infinite open-endedness only if one can speak *also* about God.

This can be demonstrated negatively: an exclusion of any kind of discourse about God from language would have to be made according to certain determined *general* criteria that hold true for *all* speech. There were attempts to arrive at such criteria through Logical Positivism[1] and in the School of Erlangen[2]. Similar attempts were made by Marxism and other forms of contemporary theoretical atheism. These criteria, however, would finally impinge upon all linguistic expressions, without which human language cannot function at all. The same is true of any logical rule which would render a religious use of language devoid of significance. Such a rule would also affect all ideologies and utopias, as well as philosophy, especially metaphysics, esthetics, morals, poetry and a good part of mathematics.

As a consequence we see that language cannot be *regulated!* All such regimentation would deprive us of the multiplexity of our speech. Even a regimentation of language would not exclude *a priori* all nonsense: the fact that we can say even something that makes no sense is the price for the fact that language is open-ended. Paradoxically one can tell a lie, speak in error, and say something senseless. One can even deny God: "Dixit insipiens: non est Deus!".[3] But this itself is possible because language is so open as to offer a place *even and also* for God. The possibility of speaking God is the guarantee for the logical freedom of the word — even for that of the atheist.

Only if one can then *really* speak about God does language remain open: where one cannot speak about God, one falls into the banality of chatter which is not *communicative,* and into slogans of ideology and propaganda that are not *informative.* To maintain the openness of language in the face of this is an imperative task. This is not to say that we should always and in all contexts be speaking about God — that would be 'linguistic integralism'. But there is a need, along with other things, to speak *also* about God. Language must be used *also* in a religious application. Only then can the openness of language itself be *expressed.*

NOTES

1. Cfr. Carlo Huber, Der Ausschluss der Theologie aus den Wissenschaften durch Sprachregelungen in der Erlanger Schule; in *Wissenschaftsbegriff und Glaube der Kirche* (Dialogsekretariat, 1978, Ms.)

2. Not all the philosophers that are recognized in the School of Erlangen — which for its logical and linguistic constructionism merits considerable attention — arrive at the conclusions of M. Gatzmeier, *Theologie als Wissenschaft* (Stuttgart-Bad Cannstatt, 1974 and 1975).

3. Psalms 13, 1 and 52, 1. Cfr. Anselm, *Prosologion* II.

INDEX

A

Anselm 73, 76, 86, 91
Aquinas 1, 30, 37, 48, 56, 80, 88
Aristotle 1, 25, 30, 46, 48

B

Belief 8, 86, 88
Bible 58, 88
Bishop 34
Blue Book 13
Bread 57, 60, 65-72
Brentano 24-25
Brown Book 13
Buber 47
Buddha 5, 7, 33

C

Carnap 48
Carroll 73, 85
Catholic 5, 8, 9, 10, 11, 12, 33, 36, 37, 87
Christian iii, 1, 2, 5-14, 21-23, 27-28, 33-39, 41-42, 44, 48-49, 55, 57-61, 69-70,
    73-75, 77-81, 85-86, 88-89
Church 8, 10, 34, 36, 41, 59, 61, 81-82, 87
Communication iii, 19, 23, 55, 57-58, 61, 68, 84, 89
Confucianism 7
Consciousness 1, 19, 24-27, 29, 68-69, 72, 74-75, 79, 81, 86
Cusanus 47-48, 55, 78, 87

D

David 47, 53, 61
DaVinci 78
Descartes 30-31, 47, 73, 86
Dionysius 47
Discourse iii, 1-2, 5-13, 21, 23, 27-28, 33-42, 48, 51, 53, 55, 73-75, 77-78, 83-84,
    88-89
Divine iii, 1, 9, 12, 47, 49, 53-54, 59

E

English 34-36
Environment 22

COUNCIL FOR RESEARCH IN
VALUES AND PHILOSOPHY
Members

THE COUNCIL FOR
RESEARCH IN VALUES AND PHILOSOPHY

PURPOSE

Today there is urgent need to attend to the nature and dignity of the person, to the quality of human life, to the purpose and goal of the physical transformation of our environment, and to the relation of all this to the development of social and political life. This, in turn, requires philosophic clarification of the base upon which freedom is exercised, that is, of the values which provide stability and guidance to one's decisions.

Such studies must be able to reach deeply into the cultures of one's nation—and of other parts of the world by which they can be strengthened and enriched—in order to uncover the roots of the dignity of persons and of the societies built upon their relations one with another. They must be able to identify the conceptual forms in terms of which modern industrial and technological developments are structured and how these impact human self-understanding. Above all, they must be able to bring these elements together in the creative understanding essential for setting our goals and determining our modes of interaction. In the present complex circumstances this is a condition for growing together with trust and justice, honest dedication and mutual concern.

The Council for Studies in Values and Philosophy (RVP) is a group of scholars who share the above concerns and are interested in the application thereto of existing capabilities in the field of philosophy and other disciplines. Its work is to identify areas in which study is needed, the intellectual resources which can be brought to bear thereupon, and the means for publication and interchange of the work from the various regions of the world. In bringing these together its goal is scientific discovery and publication which contributes to the promotion of human kind in our times.

In sum, our times present both the need and the opportunity for deeper and ever more progressive understanding of the person and of the foundations of social life. The development of such understanding is the goal of the RVP.

PROJECTS

A set of related research efforts is currently in process; some were developed initially by the RVP and others now are being carried forward by it, either solely or conjointly.

1. *Cultural Heritage and Contemporary Change: Philosophical Foundations for Social Life.* Sets of focused and mutually coordinated continuing seminars in university centers, each preparing a volume as part of an integrated philosophic search for self-understanding differentiated by continent. This work focuses upon evolving a more adequate understanding of the person in society and looks to the cultural heritage of each for the resources to respond to the challenges of its own specific contemporary transformation.

2. *Seminars on Culture and Contemporary Issues.* This series of 10 week crosscultural and interdisciplinary seminars is being coordinated by the RVP in Washington.

3. *Joint-Colloquia* with Institutes of Philosophy of the National Academies of Science, university philosophy departments, and societies, which have been underway since 1976 in Eastern Europe and, since 1987 in China, concern the person in contemporary society.

4. *Foundations of Moral Education and Character Development.* A study in values and education which unites philosophers, psycholo-gists, social scientists and scholars in education in the elaboration of ways of enriching the moral content of education and character development. This work has been underway since 1980 especially in the Americas.

The personnel for these projects consists of established scholars willing to contribute their time and research as part of their professional commitment to life in our society. For resources to implement this work the Council, as a non-profit organization incorporated in the District of Colombia, looks to various private foundations, public programs and enterprises.

PUBLICATIONS ON CULTURAL HERITAGE AND CONTEMPORARY CHANGE

Series I.	*Culture and Values*
Series II.	*Africa*
Series IIa.	*Islam*
Series III.	*Asia*
Series IV.	*W. Europe and North America*
Series IVa.	*Central and Eastern Europe*
Series V.	*Latin America*
Series VI.	*Foundations of Moral Education*

CULTURAL HERITAGE
AND CONTEMPORARY CHANGE

VALUES AND CONTEMPORARY LIFE

Series I. Culture and Values

Vol. I.12   *Ethics at the Crossroads: Vol. 2. Personalist Ethics and Human Subjectivity,*
George F. McLean,
ISBN 1-56518-024-0 (paper).

Vol. I.13   *The Emancipative Theory of Jürgen Habermas and Metaphysics,*
Robert Badillo,
ISBN 1-56518-043-7 (cloth); ISBN 1-56518-042-9 (paper).

Vol. I.14   *The Deficient Cause of Moral Evil According to Thomas Aquinas,*
Edward Cook,
ISBN 1-56518-070-4 paper (paper).

Vol. I.16   *Civil Society and Social Reconstruction,*
George F. McLean,
ISBN 1-56518-086-0 (paper).

Vol.I.17   *Ways to God, Personal and Social at the Turn of Millennia*
The Iqbal Lecture, Lahore
George F. McLean
ISBN 1-56518-123-9 (paper).

Vol.I.18   *The Role of the Sublime in Kant's Moral Metaphysics*
John R. Goodreau
ISBN 1-56518-124-7 (paper).

Vol.I .20   *Faith, Reason and Philosophy*
Lectures at The al-Azhar, Qum, Tehran, Lahore and Beijing
Appendix: The Encyclical Letter: Fides et Ratio
George F. McLean
ISBN 1-56518-1301 (paper).

Vol.I.21   *Religion and the Relation between Civilizations:*
Lectures on Cooperation between Islamic and
Christian Cultures in a Global Horizon
George F. McLean
ISBN 1-56518-152-2 (paper).

Vol.22   *Freedom, Cultural Traditions and Progress:*
Philosophy in Civil Society and Nation Building:
Tashkent Lectures, 1999
George F. McLean
ISBN 1-56518-151-4 (paper).

Vol.24   *God and the Challenge of Evil: A Critical Examination of*
Some Serious Objections to the Good and Omnipotent God
John L. Yardan
ISBN 1-56518-160-3 (paper).

Vol.26   *The Culture of Citizenship: Inventing Postmodern*
Civic Culture
Thomas Bridges
ISBN 1-56518-168-9 (paper).

Vol.28   *Speaking of God*
Carlo Huber
ISBN 1-56518-169-7 (paper).

CULTURAL HERITAGES AND
THE FOUNDATIONS OF SOCIAL LIFE

Series II. Africa

Vol. II.1   *Person and Community: Ghanaian Philosophical Studies: I,*
Kwasi Wiredu and Kwame Gyeke,
ISBN 1-56518-005-4 (cloth); ISBN 1-56518-004-6 (paper).
Vol. II.2   *The Foundations of Social Life:*
Ugandan Philosophical Studies: I,
A.T. Dalfovo,
ISBN 1-56518-007-0 (cloth); ISBN 1-56518-006-2 (paper).
Vol. II.3   *Identity and Change in Nigeria:*
Nigerian Philosophical Studies, I,
Theophilus Okere,
ISBN 1-56518-068-2 (paper).
Vol. II.4   *Social Reconstruction in Africa:*
Ugandan Philosophical studies, II
E. Wamala, A.R. Byaruhanga, A.T. Dalfovo,
J.K. Kigongo, S.A. Mwanahewa and G. Tusabe
ISBN 1-56518-118-2 (paper).
Vol. II.5   *Ghana: Changing Values/Chaning Technologies:*
Ghanaian Philosophical Studies, II
Helen Lauer
ISBN 1-56518-1441 (paper).
Vol.II.6   *Sameness and Difference: Problems and Potentials in South African Civil Society: South African Philosophical Studies, I*
James R. Cochrane and Bastienne Klein
ISBN 1-56518-155-7 (paper).

Series IIA. Islam

Vol. IIA.1   *Islam and the Political Order,*
Muhammad Saïd al-Ashmawy,
ISBN 1-56518-046-1 (cloth); ISBN 1-56518-047-x (paper).
Vol. IIA.3   *Philosophy in Pakistan*
Naeem Ahmad
ISBN 1-56518-108-5 (paper).
Vol. IIA.4   *The Authenticity of the Text in Hermeneutics*
Seyed Musa Dibadj

ISBN 1-56518-117-4 (paper).

Vol. IIA.5 *Interpretation and the Problem of*
the Intention of the Author: H.-G. Gadamer vs E.D. Hirsch
Burhanettin Tatar
ISBN 1-56518-121 (paper).

Vol.IAI.6 *Ways to God, Personal and Social at the Turn of Millennia*
The Iqbal Lecture, Lahore
George F. McLean
ISBN 1-56518-123-9 (paper).

Vol.I .7 *Faith, Reason and Philosophy*
Lectures at The al-Azhar, Qum, Tehran, Lahore and Beijing
Appendix: The Encyclical Letter: Fides et Ratio
George F. McLean
ISBN 1-56518-130-1 (paper).

Vol.IIA.8 *Islamic and Christian Cultures: Conflict or Dialogue:*
Bulgarian Philosophical Studies, III
Plament Makariev
ISBN 1-56518-162-X (paper).

Vol.IIA.10 *Christian-Islamic Preambles of Faith*
Joseph Kenny
ISBN 1-56518-138-7 (paper).

Vol.IIA.12 *Religion and the Relation between Civilizations:*
Lectures on Cooperation between Islamic and
Christian Cultures in a Global Horizon
George F. McLean
ISBN 1-56518-152-2 (paper).

Series III. Asia

Vol. III.1 *Man and Nature: Chinese Philosophical Studies, I,*
Tang Yi-jie, Li Zhen,
ISBN 0-8191-7412-2 (cloth); ISBN 0-8191-7413-0 (paper).

Vol. III.2 *Chinese Foundations for Moral Education and*
Character Development, Chinese Philosophical Studies, II.
Tran van Doan,
ISBN 1-56518-033-x (cloth); ISBN 1-56518-032-1 (paper).

Vol. III.3 *Confucianism, Buddhism, Taoism, Christianity and*
Chinese Culture, Chinese Philosophical Studies, III,
Tang Yijie,
ISBN 1-56518-035-6 (cloth); ISBN 1-56518-034-8 (paper).

Vol. III.4 *Morality, Metaphysics and Chinese Culture*
(Metaphysics, Culture and Morality, Vol. I)
Vincent Shen and Tran van Doan,
ISBN 1-56518-026-7 (cloth); ISBN 1-56518-027-5 (paper).

Vol. III.5 *Tradition, Harmony and Transcendence,*

George F. McLean,
ISBN 1-56518-030-5 (cloth); ISBN 1-56518-031-3 (paper).

Vol. III.6   *Psychology, Phenomenology and Chinese Philosophy:*
Chinese Philosophical Studies, VI,
Vincent Shen, Richard Knowles and Tran Van Doan,
ISBN 1-56518-044-5 (cloth); 1-56518-045-3 (paper).

Vol. III.7   *Values in Philippine Culture and Education:*
Philippine Philosophical Studies, I,
Manuel B. Dy, Jr.,
ISBN 1-56518-040-2 (cloth); 1-56518-041-2 (paper).

Vol. III.7A   *The Human Person and Society: Chinese*
Philosophical Studies, VIIA,
Zhu Dasheng, Jin Xiping and George F. McLean
ISBN 1-56518-087-9 (library edition); 1-56518-088-7 (paper).

Vol. III.8   *The Filipino Mind: Philippine Philosophical Studies II,*
Leonardo N. Mercado
ISBN 1-56518-063-1 (cloth); ISBN 1-56518-064-X (paper).

Vol. III.9   *Philosophy of Science and Education:*
Chinese Philosophical Studies IX,
Vincent Shen and Tran Van Doan
ISBN 1-56518-075-5 (cloth); 1-56518-076-3 (paper).

Vol. III.10   *Chinese Cultural Traditions and Modernization:*
Chinese Philosophical Studies, X,
Wang Miaoyang, Yu Xuanmeng and George F. McLean
ISBN 1-56518-067-4 (library edition); 1-56518-068-2 (paper).

Vol. III.11   *The Humanization of Technology and Chinese Culture:*
Chinese Philosophical Studies XI,
Tomonobu Imamichi, Wang Miaoyang and Liu Fangtong
ISBN 1-56518-116-6 (paper).

Vol. III.12   *Beyond Modernization: Chinese Roots of Global*
Awareness: Chinese Philosophical Studies, XII,
Wang Miaoyang, Yu Xuanmeng and George F. McLean
ISBN 1-56518-089-5 (library edition); 1-56518-090-9 (paper).

Vol. III.13   *Philosophy and Modernization in China:*
Chinese Philosophical Studies XIII,
Liu Fangtong, Huang Songjie and George F. McLean
ISBN 1-56518-066-6 (paper).

Vol. III.14   *Economic Ethics and Chinese Culture:*
Chinese Philosophical Studies, XIV,
Yu Xuanmeng, Lu Xiaohe, Liu Fangtong,
Zhang Rulun and Georges Enderle
ISBN 1-56518-091-7 (library edition); 1-56518-092-5 (paper).

Vol. III.15   *Civil Society in a Chinese Context:*
Chinese Philosophical Studies XV,
Wang Miaoyang, Yu Xuanmeng and Manuel B. Dy

ISBN 1-56518-084-4 (paper).
Vol. III.16   T*he Bases of Values in a Time of Change:*
Chinese and Western: Chinese Philosophical Studies, XVI
Kirti Bunchua, Liu Fangtong, Yu Xuanmeng, Yu Wujin
ISBN 1-56518-114-X (paper).
Vol. IIIB.1   *Authentic Human Destiny: The Paths of*
 Shankara and Heidegger: Indian Philosophical Studies, I
Vensus A. George
ISBN 1-56518-119-0 (paper).
 Vol. IIIB.2   *The Experience of Being as Goal of Human Existence:*
The Heideggerian Approach: Indian Philosophical Studies, II
Vensus A. George
ISBN 1-56518-145-X (paper).
Vol. IIIB.3   *Self-Realization [Brahmaanubhava]:*
The Advaitic Perspective of Shankara:
Indian Philosophical Studies, III
Vensus A. George
ISBN 1-56518-154-9 (paper).
Vol. IIIB.5   *Gandhi: The Meaning of Mahatma for the Millennium*
Indian Philosophical Studies, V
Kuruvilla Pandikattu
ISBN 1-56518-156-5 (paper).
Vol. IIIB.6   *Civil Society in Indian Cultures*
Indian Philosophical Studies, VI
Asha Mukherjee, Sabujkali Sen (Mitra) and K. Bagchi
ISBN 1-56518-157-3 (paper).
Vol. IIIC.1   *Spiritual Values and Social Progress*
Uzbekistan Philosophical Studies, I
Said Shermukhamedov and Victoriya Levinskaya
ISBN 1-56518-143-3 (paper).

Series IV. Western Europe and North America

Vol. IV.1   *Italy in Transition: The Long Road from the First to*
the Second Republic: The 1997 Edmund D. Pellegrino Lecture
on Contemporary Italian Politics
Paolo Janni
ISBN 1-56518-120-4 (paper).
Vol. IV.2   *Italy and The European Monetary Union: The 1997 Edmund*
D. Pellegrino Lecture on Contemporary Italian Politics
Paolo Janni
ISBN 1-56518-128-X (paper).
Vol. IV.3   *Italy at the Millennium: Economy, Politics, Literature*
and Journalism: The 1997 Edmund D. Pellegrino Lecture

on *Contemporary Italian Politics*
Paolo Janni
ISBN 1-56518-158-1 (paper).
Vol.4   *Speaking of God*
Carlo Huber
ISBN 1-56518-169-7 (paper).

Series IVA. Central and Eastern Europe

Vol. IVA.1   *The Philosophy of Person: Solidarity and Cultural Creativity: Polish Philosophical Studies, I,*
A. Tischner, J.M. Zycinski,
ISBN 1-56518-048-8 (cloth); ISBN 1-56518-049-6 (paper).

Vol. IVA.2   *Public and Private Social Inventions in Modern Societies: Polish   Philosophical Studies, II,*
L. Dyczewski, P. Peachey, J. Kromkowski,
ISBN 1-56518-050-x (cloth). paper ISBN 1-56518-051-8 (paper).

Vol. IVA.3   *Traditions and Present Problems of Czech Political Culture: Czechoslovak Philosophical Studies, I,*
M. Bednár, M. Vejraka
ISBN 1-56518-056-9 (cloth); ISBN 1-56518-057-7 (paper).

Vol. IVA.4   *Czech Philosophy in the XXth Century: Czech Philosophical Studies, II,*
Lubomír Nový and Jiri Gabriel,
ISBN 1-56518-028-3 (cloth); ISBN 1-56518-029-1 (paper).

Vol. IVA.5   *Language, Values and the Slovak Nation: Slovak Philosophical Studies, I,*
Tibor Pichler and Jana Gašparíková,
ISBN 1-56518-036-4 (cloth); ISBN 1-56518-037-2 (paper).

Vol. IVA.6   *Morality and Public Life in a Time of Change: Bulgarian Philosophical Studies, I,*
V. Prodanov, M. Stoyanova,
ISBN 1-56518-054-2 (cloth); ISBN 1-56518-055-0 (paper).

Vol. IVA.7   *Knowledge and Morality: Georgian PhilosophicalStudies, I,*
N.V. Chavchavadze, G. Nodia, P. Peachey,
ISBN 1-56518-052-6 (cloth); ISBN 1-56518-053-4 (paper).

Vol. IVA.8   *Cultural Heritage and Social Change: Lithuanian Philosophical Studies, I,*
Bronius Kuzmickas and Aleksandr Dobrynin,
ISBN 1-56518-038-0 (cloth); ISBN 1-56518-039-9 (paper).

Vol. IVA.9   *National, Cultural and Ethnic Identities: Harmony beyond Conflict: Czech Philosophical Studies, IV*
Jaroslav Hroch, David Hollan, George F. McLean
ISBN 1-56518-113-1 (paper).

Vol. IVA.10   *Models of Identities in Postcommunist Societies:*
Yugoslav Philosophical Studies, I
Zagorka Golubovic and George F. McLean
ISBN 1-56518-121-1 (paper).

Vol. IVA.11   *Interests and Values: The Spirit of Venture in*
a Time of Change: Slovak Philosophical Studies, II
Tibor Pichler and Jana Gasparikova
ISBN 1-56518-125-5 (paper).

Vol. IVA.12   *Creating Democratic Societies: Values and Norms;*
Bulgarian Philosophical Studies, II
Plamen Makariev, Andrew M. Blasko, Asen Davidov
ISBN 1-56518-131-X (paper).

Vol. IVA.14   *Values and Education in Romania Today;*
Romanian Philosophical Studies, I
Marin Calin and Magdalena Dumitrana
ISBN 1-56518-134-4 (paper).

Vol. IVA.16   *Culture and Freedom;*
Romanian Philosophical Studies, III
Marin Aiftinca
ISBN 1-56518-136-0 (paper).

Vol. IVA.17   *Lithuanian Philosophy: Persons and Ideas*
Lithuanian Philosophical Studies, II
Jurate Baranova
ISBN 1-56518-137-9 (paper).

Vol. IVA.18   *Human Dignity: Values and Justice;*
Czech Philosophical Studies, III
Miloslav Bednar
ISBN 1-56518-1409 (paper).

Vol.IVA.21   *Islamic and Christian Cultures: Conflict or Dialogue:*
Bulgarian Philosophical Studies, III
Plament Makariev
ISBN 1-56518-162-X (paper).

Series V. Latin America

Vol. V.1   *The Social Context and Values: Perspectives of*
the Americas,
O. Pegoraro,
ISBN 0-8191-7354-1 (cloth); ISBN 0-8191-7355-x (paper).

Vol. V.2   *Culture, Human Rights and Peace in Central America,*
Raul Molina, Timothy Ready,
ISBN 0-8191-7356-8 (cloth); ISBN 0-8191-7357-6 (paper).

Vol V.3   *El Cristianismo Aymara: Inculturacion o culturizacion?,*
Luis Jolicoeur
ISBN 1-56518-104-2 (paper).

Vol. V.4   *Love as theFoundation of Moral Education and
            Character Development*
            Luis Ugalde, Nicolas Barros, George F. McLean
            ISBN 1-56518-080-1 (paper).
Vol. V.5   *Human Rights, Solidarity and Subsidiarity:
            Essays towards a Social Ontology*
            Carlos E. A. Maldonado
            ISBN 1-56518-110-7 (paper).

FOUNDATIONS OF MORAL EDUCATION
AND CHARACTER DEVELOPMENT

Series VI. Foundations of Moral Education

Vol. VI.1   *Philosophical Foundations for Moral Education and
            Character Development: Act and Agent,*
            G. McLean, F. Ellrod,
            ISBN 1-56518-001-1 (cloth); ISBN 1-56518-000-3 (paper).
Vol. VI.2   *Psychological Foundations for Moral Education and
            Character Development: An Integrated Theory of
            Moral Development,*
            R. Knowles,
            ISBN 1-56518-003-8 (cloth); ISBN 1-56518-002-x (paper).
Vol. VI.3   *Character Development in Schools and Beyond,*
            Kevin Ryan, Thomas Lickona,
            ISBN 1-56518-058-5 (cloth); ISBN 1-56518-059-3 (paper).
Vol. VI.4   *The Social Context and Values: Perspectives of
            the Americas,*
            O. Pegoraro,
            ISBN 0-8191-7354-1 (cloth); ISBN 0-8191-7355-x (paper).
Vol. VI.5   *Chinese Foundations for Moral Education and
            Character Development,*
            Tran van Doan,
            ISBN 1-56518-033 (cloth), ISBN 1-56518-032-1 (paper).

The International Society for Metaphysics

Vol.1   *Person and Nature*
         George F. McLean and Hugo Meynell, eds.
         ISBN 0-8191-7025-9 (cloth); ISBN 0-8191-7026-7 (paper).
Vol.2   *Person and Society*
         George F. McLean and Hugo Meynell, eds.
         ISBN 0-8191-6924-2 (cloth); ISBN 0-8191-6925-0 (paper).
Vol.3   *Person and God*
         George F. McLean and Hugo Meynell, eds.

ISBN 0-8191-6937-4 (cloth); ISBN 0-8191-6938-2 (paper).
Vol.4   *The Nature of Metaphysical Knowledge*
George F. McLean and Hugo Meynell, eds.
ISBN 0-8191-6926-9 (cloth); ISBN 0-8191-6927-7 (paper).

The series is published and distributed by: The Council for Research in Values and Philosophy, Cardinal Station, P.O. Box 261, Washington, D.C. 20064, Tel./Fax. 202/319-6089; e-mail: cua-rvp@cua.edu; website: http://www.crvp.org

Prices: -- Europe and North America: cloth $45.00; paper $17.50; plus shipping: surface, $3.50 first volume; $1.00 each additional; UPS, $5.50 first copy; air, $7.20. -- Latin American and Afro-Asian editions: $4.00 per volume; plus shipping: sea, $1.75; air, Latin America $5.70; Afro-Asia: $9.00.